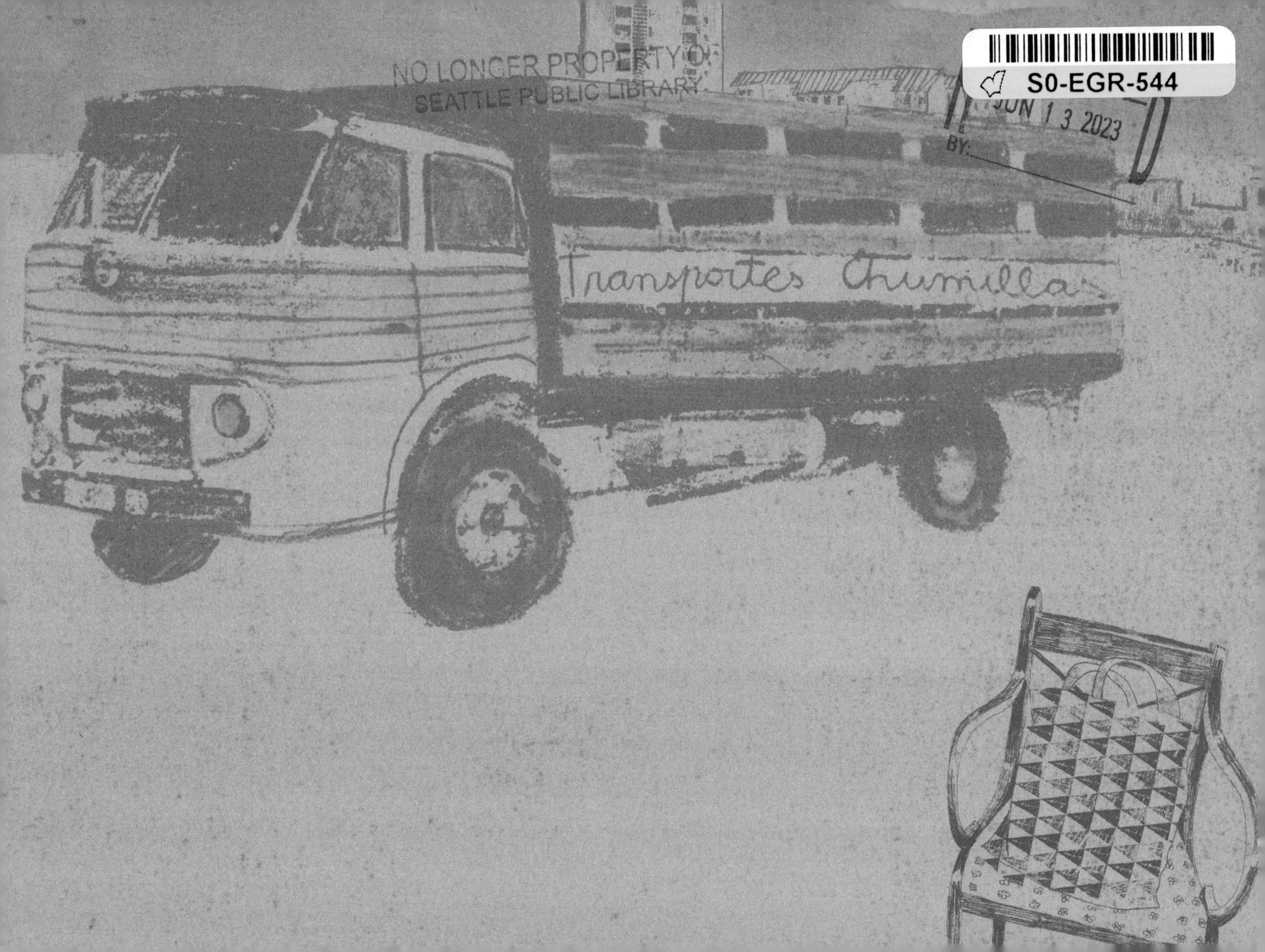
Transportes Chumilla

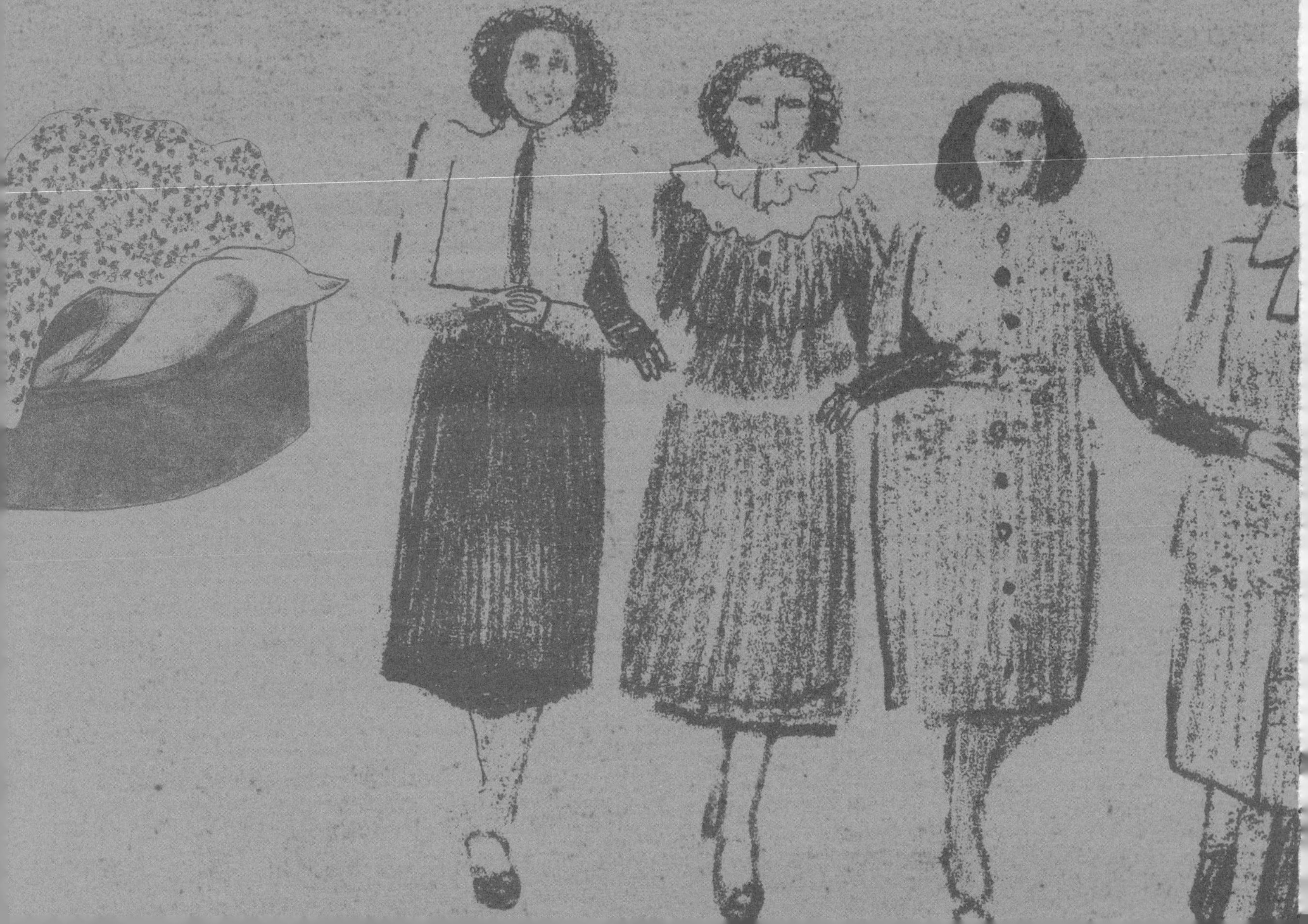

". . . THOSE CLASSIC PENELOPES, CONDEMNED TO SEWING, SITTING QUIETLY, AND WAITING. SEWING AS THEY WAITED FOR A SUITOR TO FALL FROM THE HEAVENS. THEN, LATER, IF THE SUITOR HAD APPEARED, SEWING AS A WAY TO PASS THE TIME WHILE WAITING FOR THE WEDDING. . . . AND STILL SEWING, FINALLY, ONCE HE'D GONE FROM SUITOR TO HUSBAND, WAITING WITH THE SWEETEST FORGIVING SMILE FOR HIS LATE RETURN HOME."

—CARMEN MARTÍN GAITE

We're All
Just Fine

TRANSLATOR: ANDREA ROSENBERG
DESIGNER: KAYLA E.
EDITOR: CONRAD GROTH
PRODUCTION: C HWANG
PUBLICITY: JACQ COHEN
VP / ASSOCIATE PUBLISHER: ERIC REYNOLDS
PRESIDENT / PUBLISHER: GARY GROTH

THIS BOOK WAS TRANSLATED FROM SPANISH BY ANDREA ROSENBERG WITH THE SUPPORT
OF ACCIÓN CULTURAL ESPAÑOLA (AC/E) (HTTP://WWW.ACCIONCULTURAL.ES/)

AC/E
ACCIÓN CULTURAL
ESPAÑOLA

FANTAGRAPHICS BOOKS, INC.
7563 LAKE CITY WAY NE
SEATTLE, WA 98115
WWW.FANTAGRAPHICS.COM
@FANTAGRAPHICS

ISBN: 978-1-68396-580-0
LIBRARY OF CONGRESS CONTROL NUMBER: 2022941928
FIRST FANTAGRAPHICS BOOKS EDITION: WINTER 2023
PRINTED IN CHINA

We're all just fine

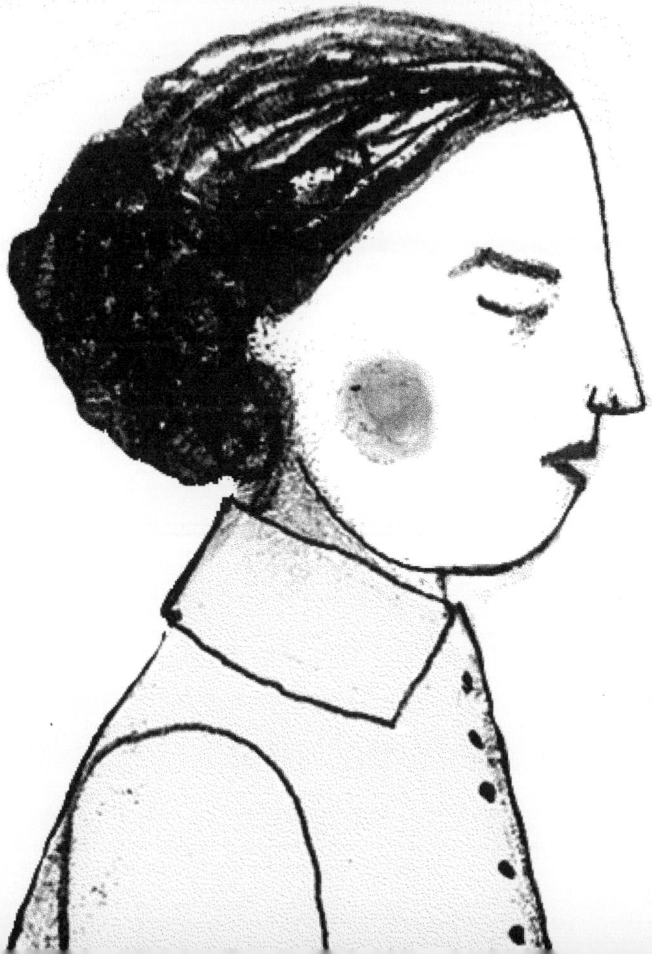

Ana Penyas

Translated by
Andrea Rosenberg

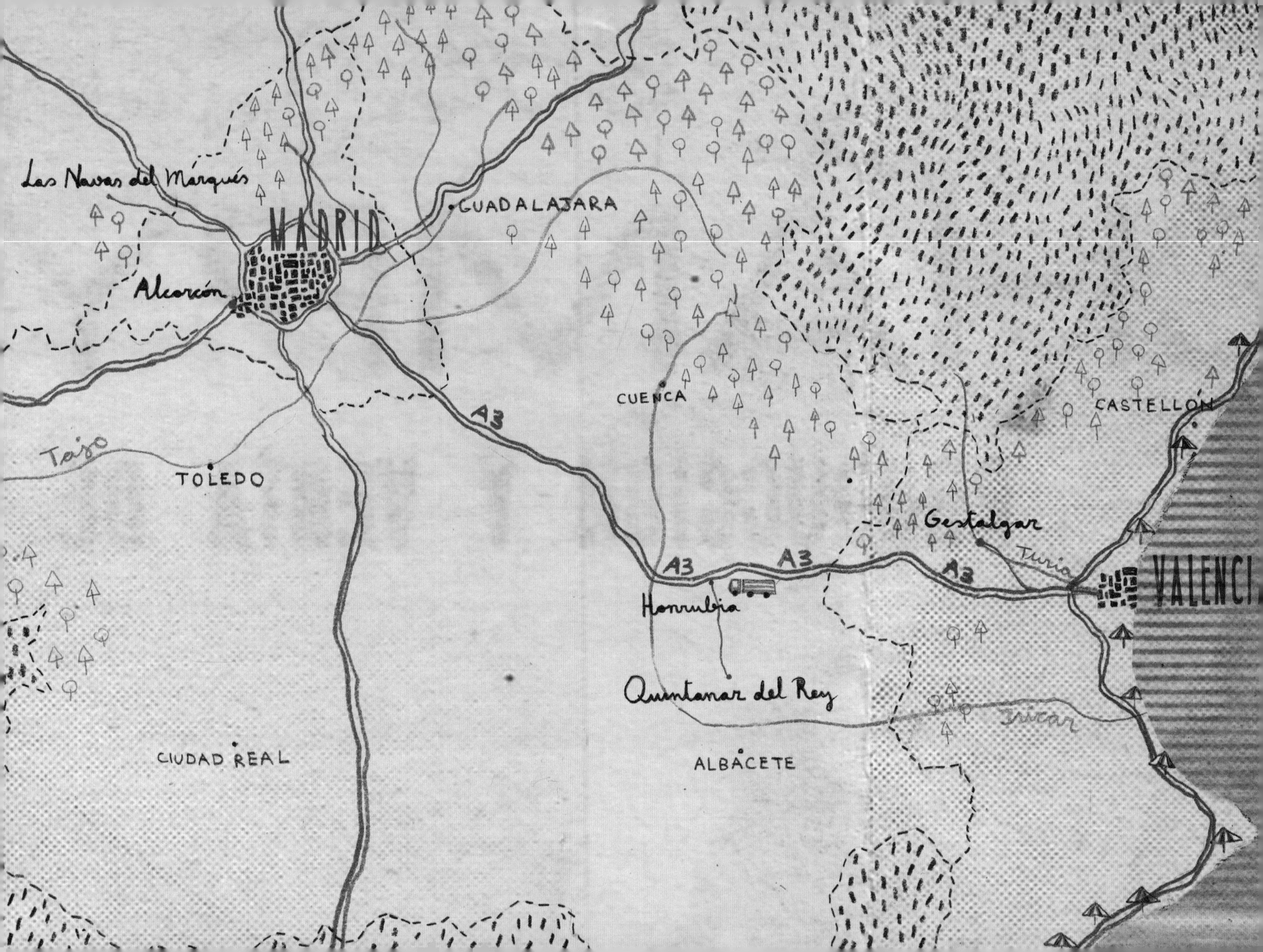
Las Navas del Marqués
MADRID
Alcorcón
GUADALAJARA
CUENCA
A3
Tajo
TOLEDO
CASTELLON
Gestalgar
Turia
A3
A3
A3
VALENCI
Honrubia
Quintanar del Rey
CIUDAD REAL
ALBACETE

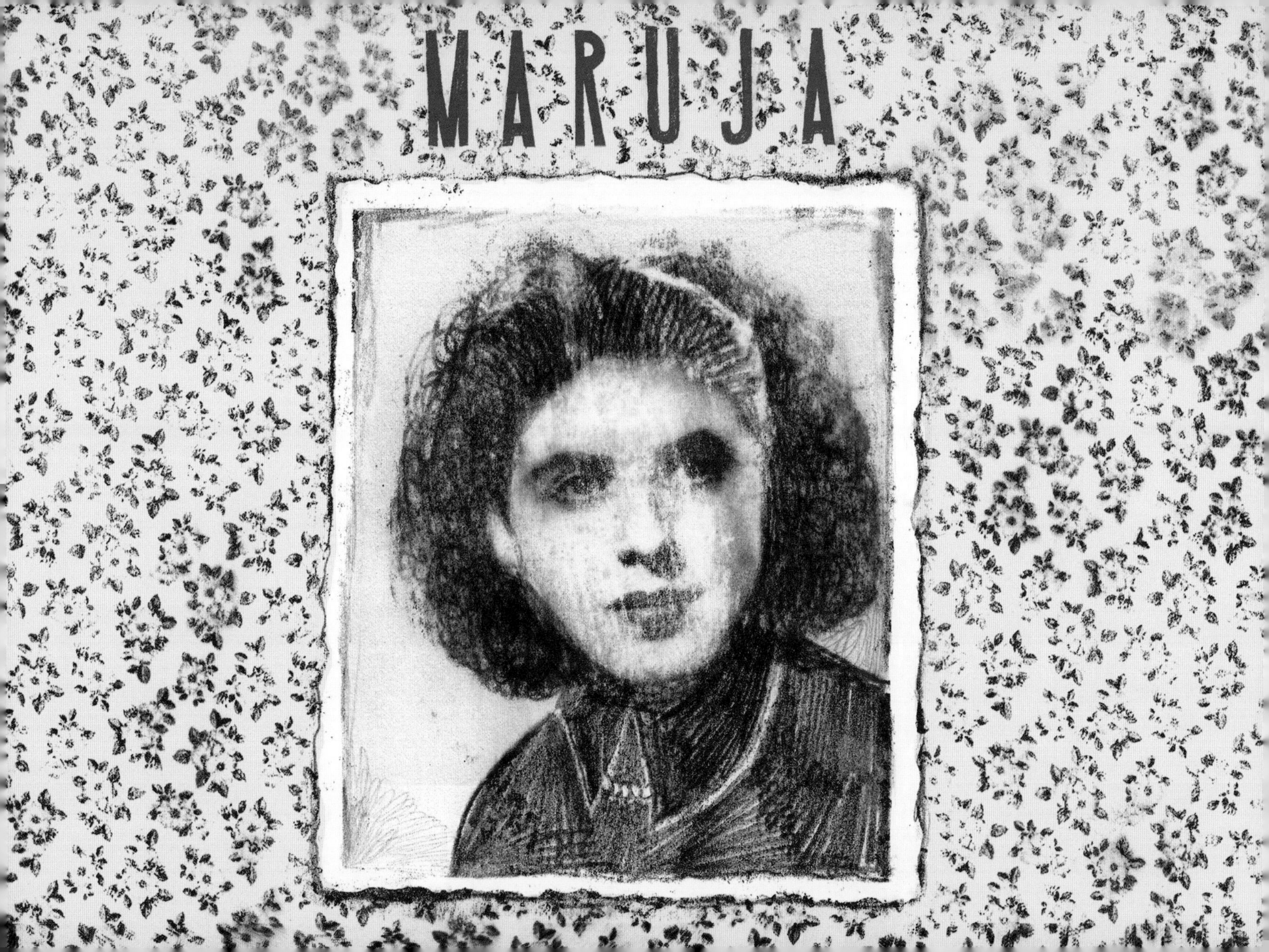
MARUJA

[GIVE IT YOUR ALL, LADIES!]

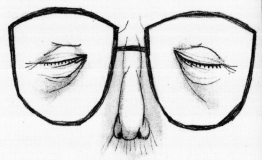

[WHO DO YOU THINK WON?]

[I'M GETTING HOT FLASHES!]

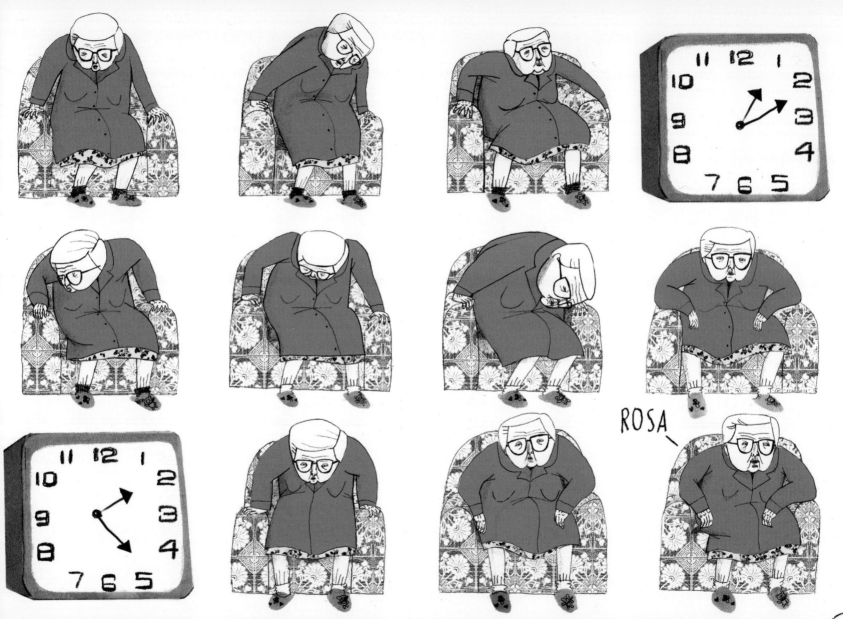

ROSA

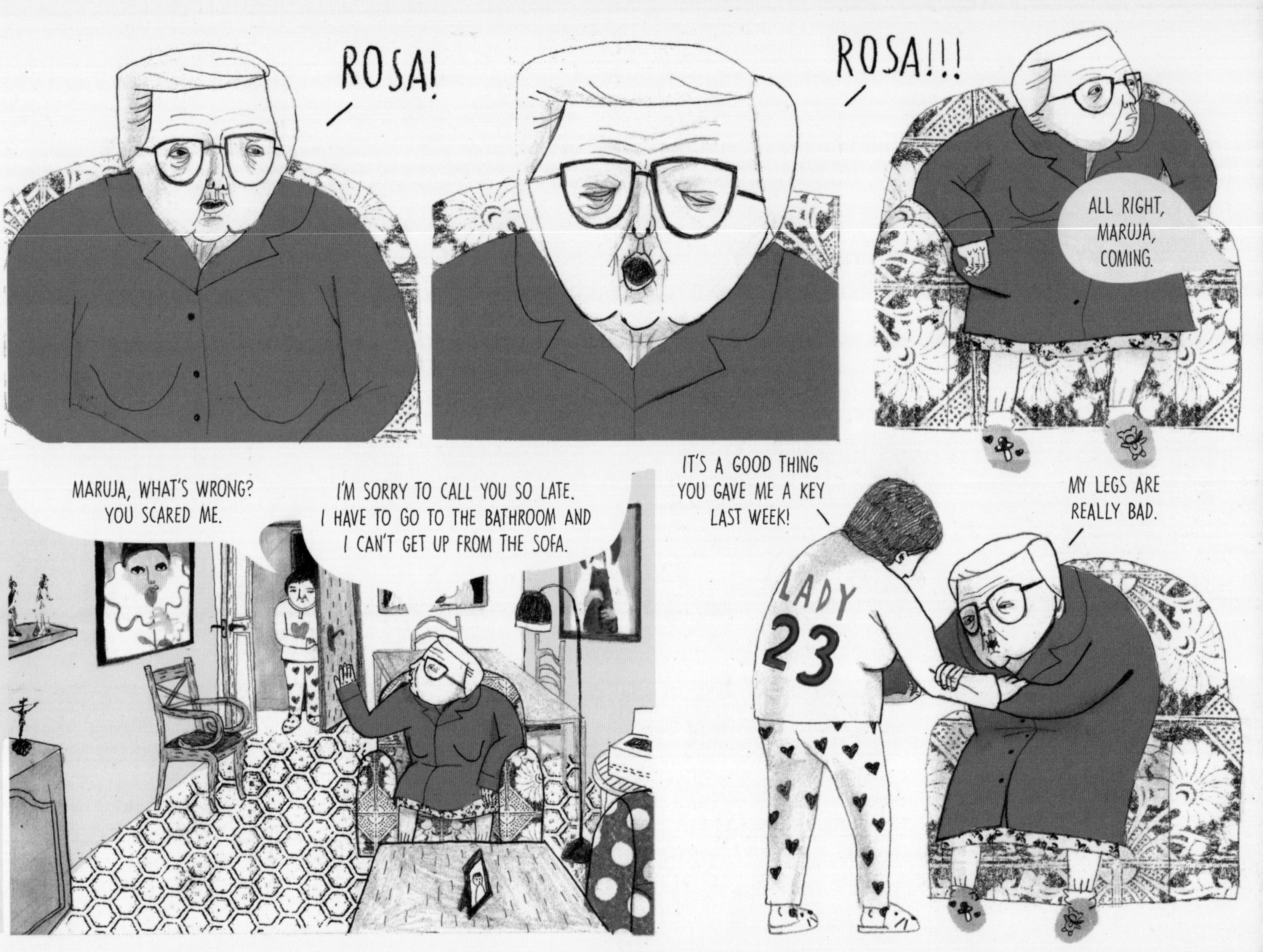
ROSA!
ROSA!!!
ALL RIGHT, MARUJA, COMING.
MARUJA, WHAT'S WRONG? YOU SCARED ME.
I'M SORRY TO CALL YOU SO LATE. I HAVE TO GO TO THE BATHROOM AND I CAN'T GET UP FROM THE SOFA.
IT'S A GOOD THING YOU GAVE ME A KEY LAST WEEK!
MY LEGS ARE REALLY BAD.
LADY
23

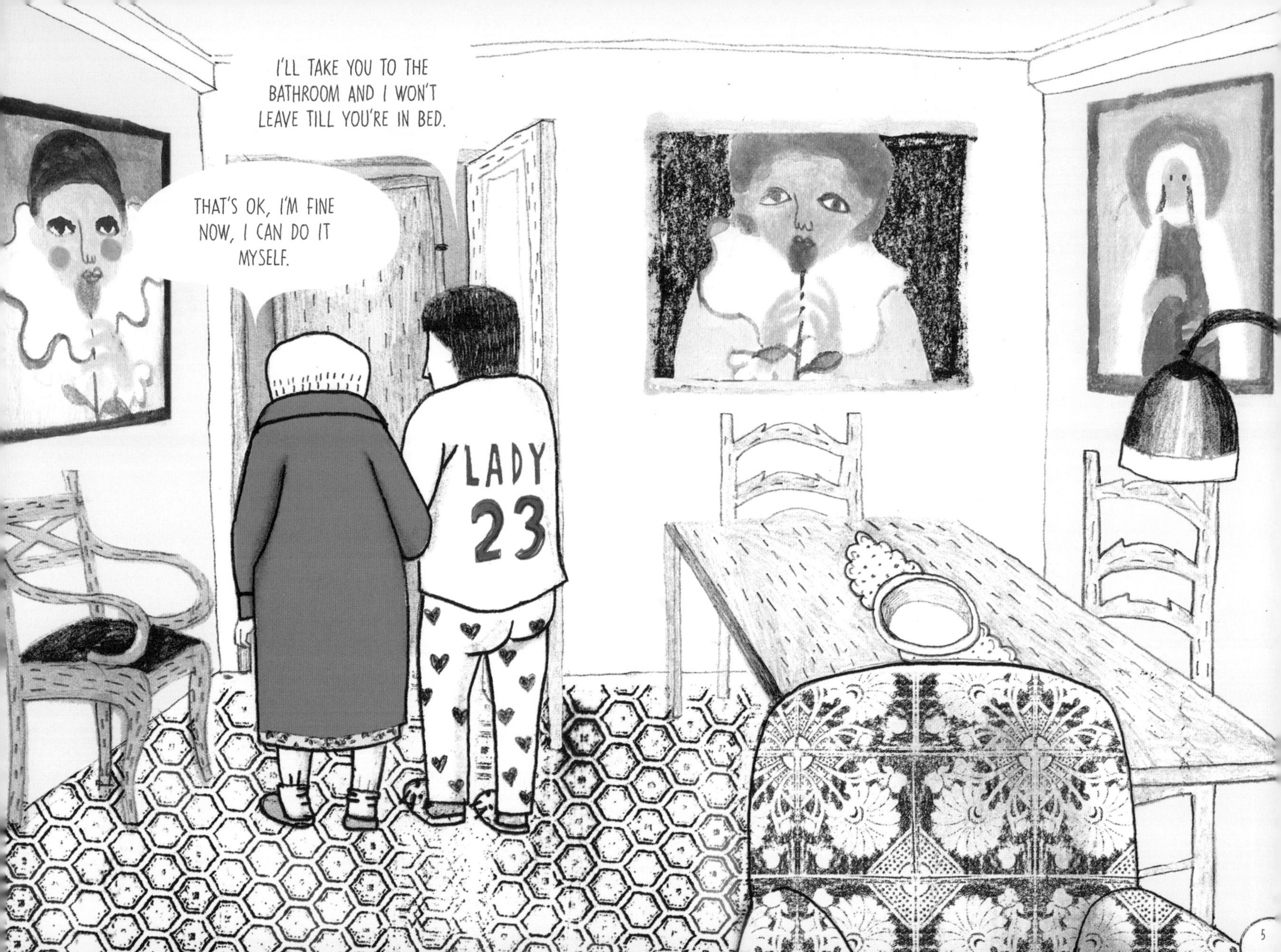
I'LL TAKE YOU TO THE BATHROOM AND I WON'T LEAVE TILL YOU'RE IN BED.
THAT'S OK, I'M FINE NOW, I CAN DO IT MYSELF.
LADY 23

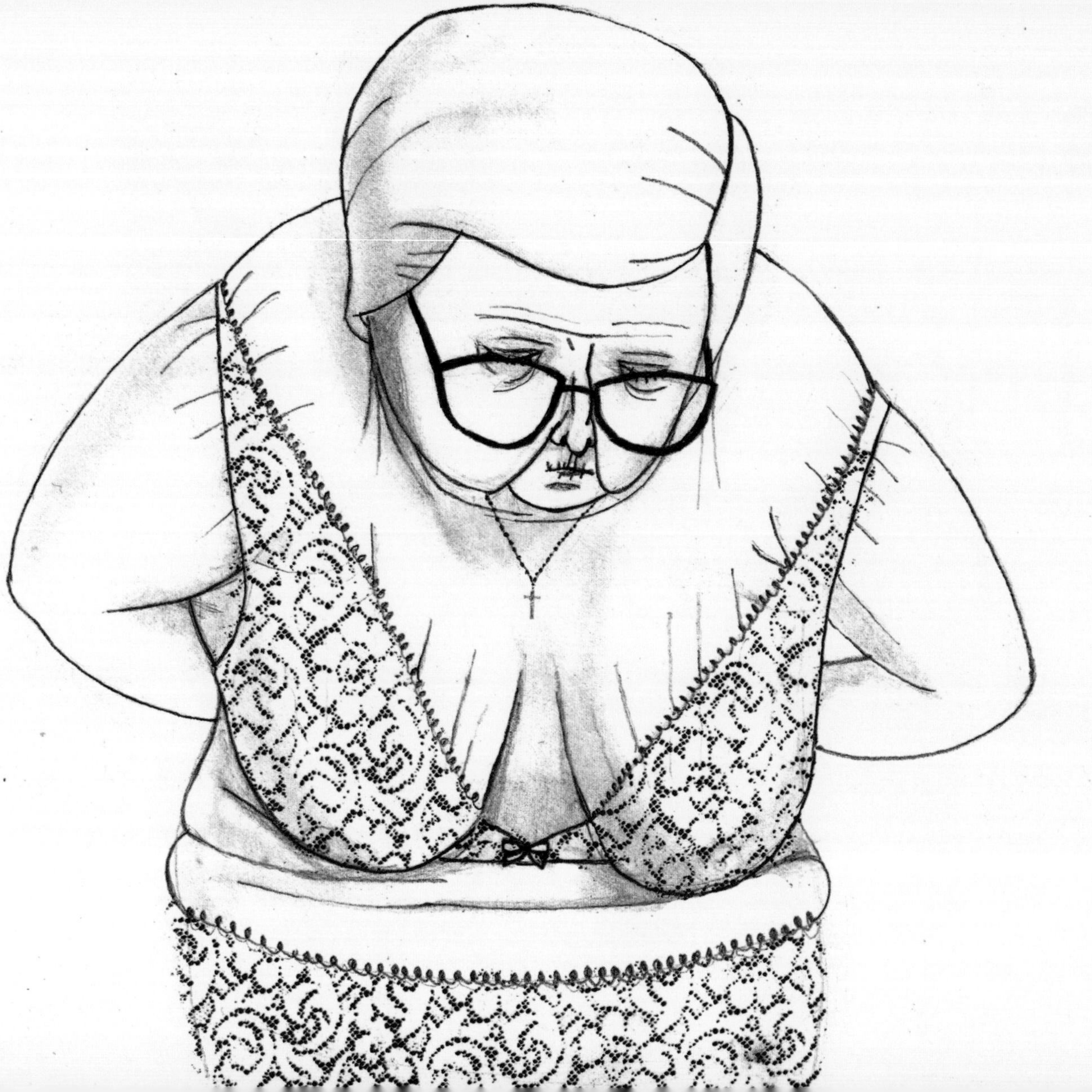

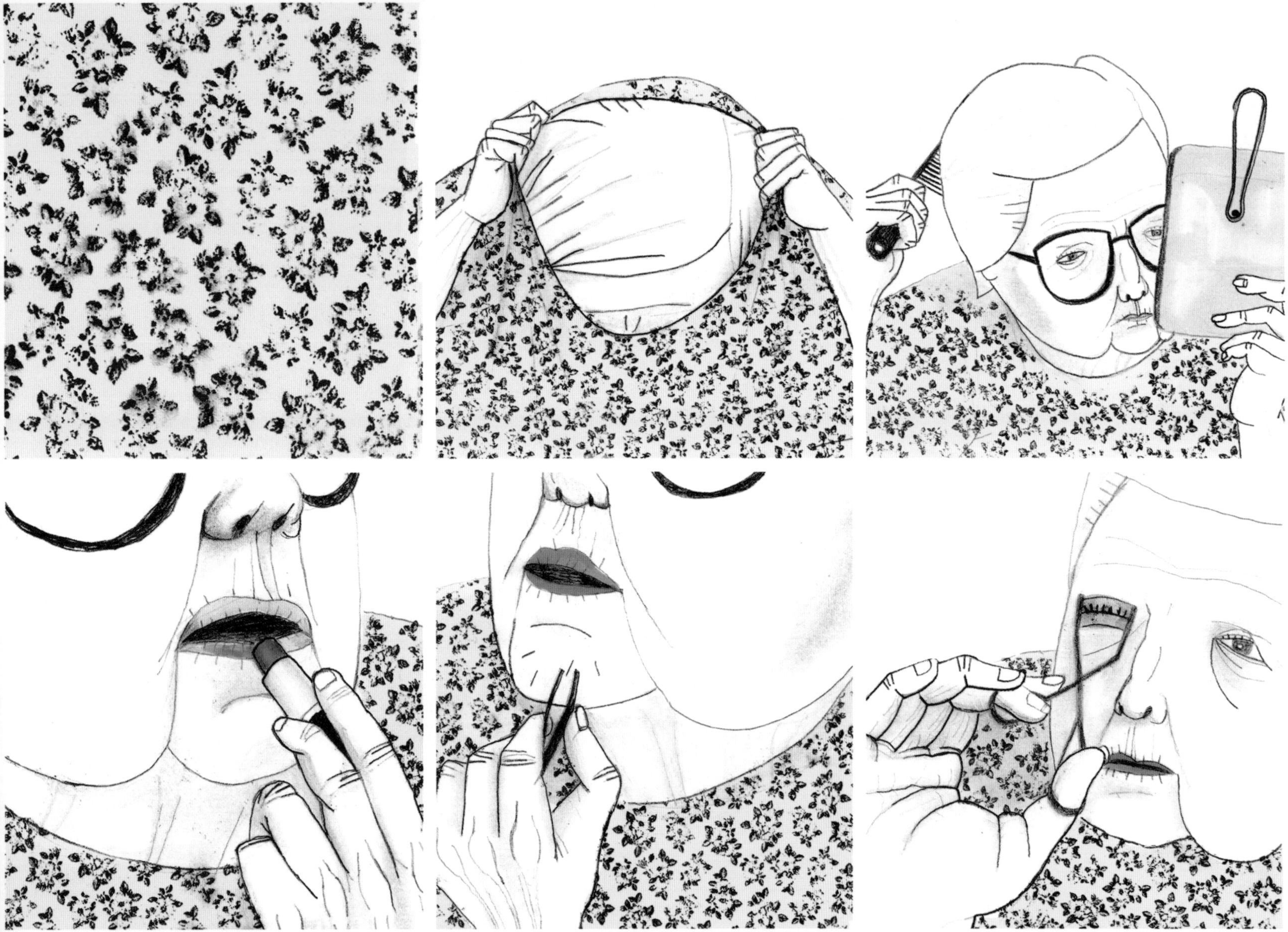

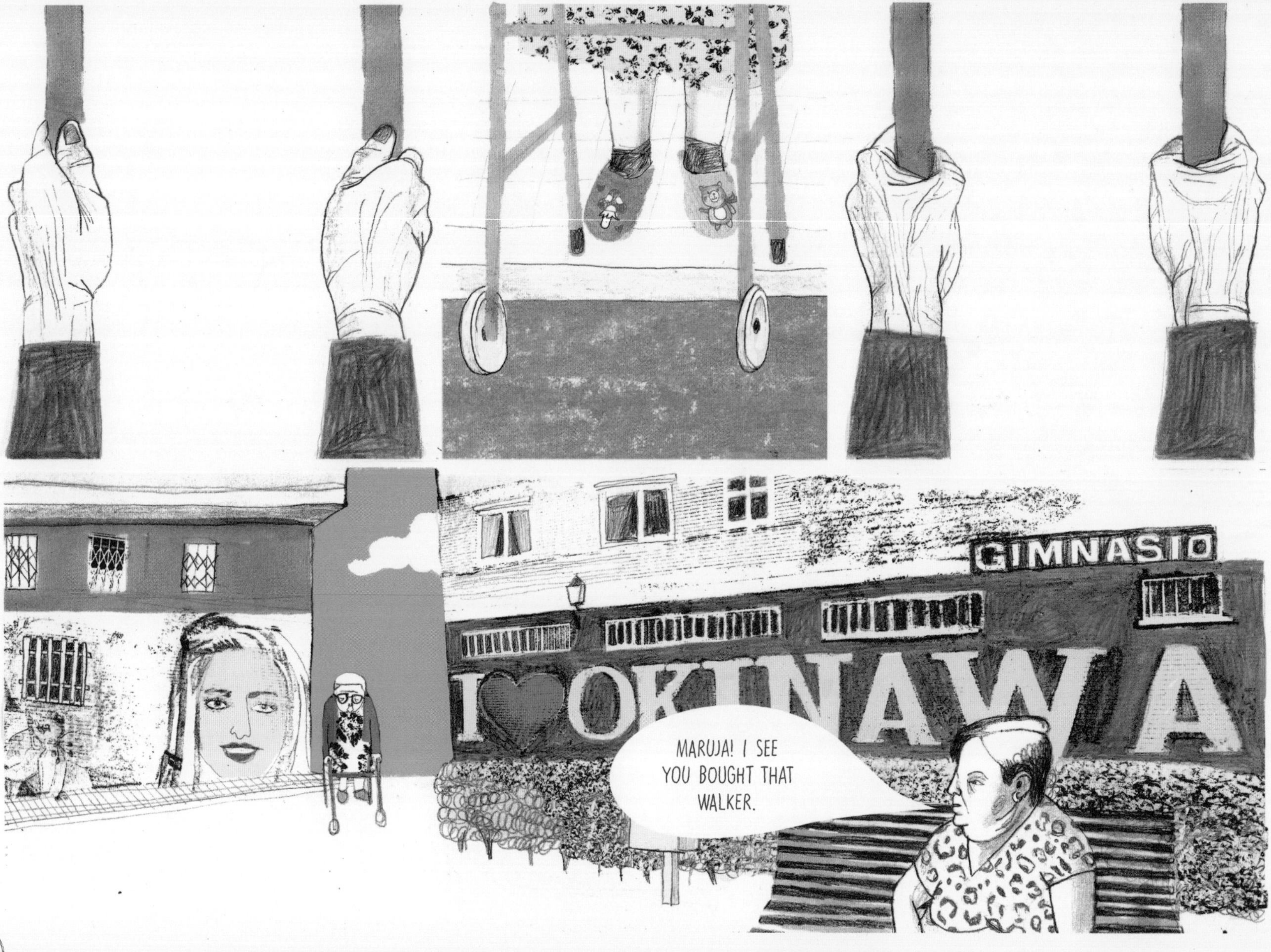
GIMNASIO
I ♥ OKINAWA
MARUJA! I SEE YOU BOUGHT THAT WALKER.

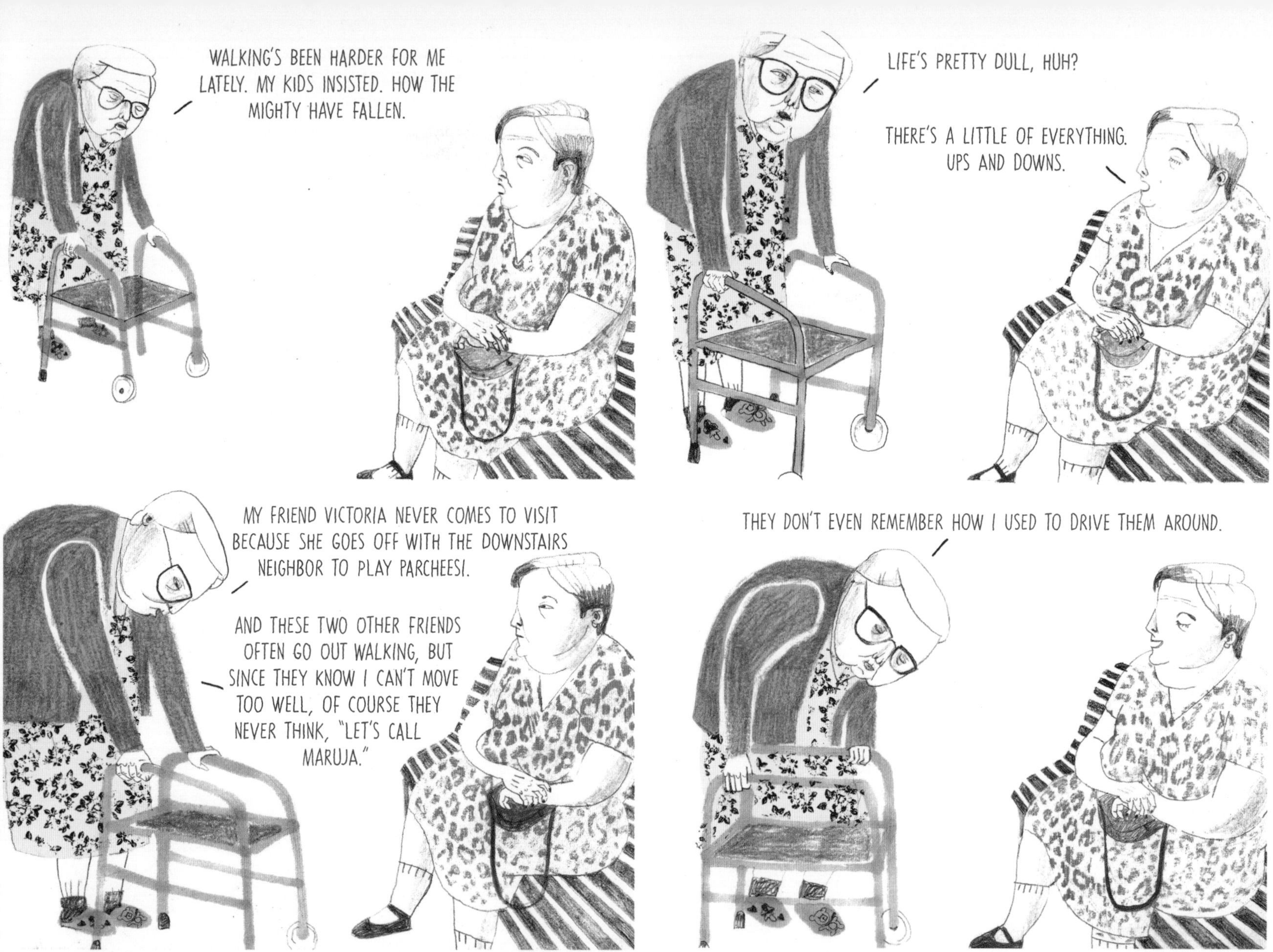
WALKING'S BEEN HARDER FOR ME LATELY. MY KIDS INSISTED. HOW THE MIGHTY HAVE FALLEN.
LIFE'S PRETTY DULL, HUH?
THERE'S A LITTLE OF EVERYTHING. UPS AND DOWNS.
MY FRIEND VICTORIA NEVER COMES TO VISIT BECAUSE SHE GOES OFF WITH THE DOWNSTAIRS NEIGHBOR TO PLAY PARCHEESI.
AND THESE TWO OTHER FRIENDS OFTEN GO OUT WALKING, BUT SINCE THEY KNOW I CAN'T MOVE TOO WELL, OF COURSE THEY NEVER THINK, "LET'S CALL MARUJA."
THEY DON'T EVEN REMEMBER HOW I USED TO DRIVE THEM AROUND.

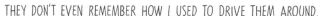

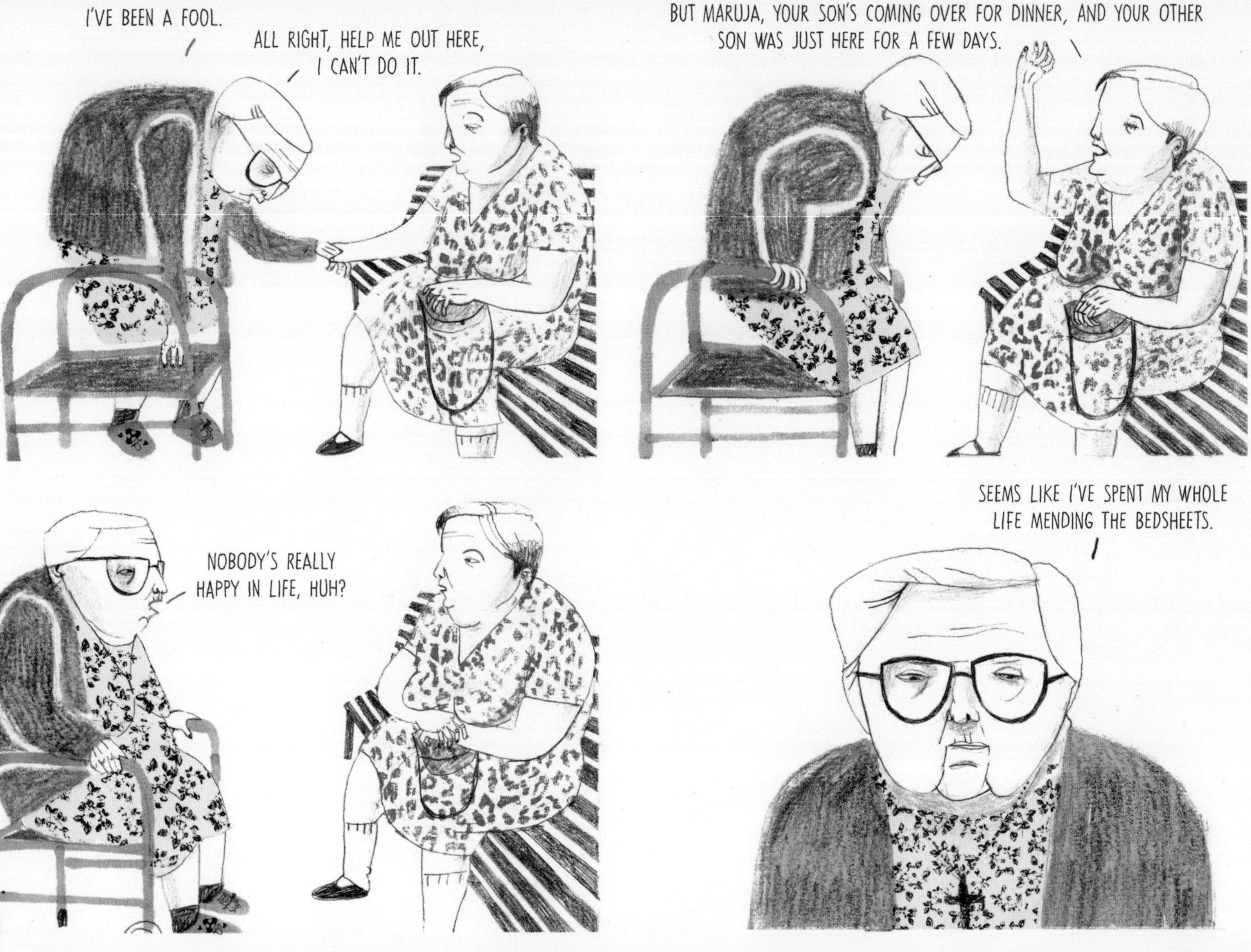
I'VE BEEN A FOOL.
ALL RIGHT, HELP ME OUT HERE, I CAN'T DO IT.
BUT MARUJA, YOUR SON'S COMING OVER FOR DINNER, AND YOUR OTHER SON WAS JUST HERE FOR A FEW DAYS.
NOBODY'S REALLY HAPPY IN LIFE, HUH?
SEEMS LIKE I'VE SPENT MY WHOLE LIFE MENDING THE BEDSHEETS.

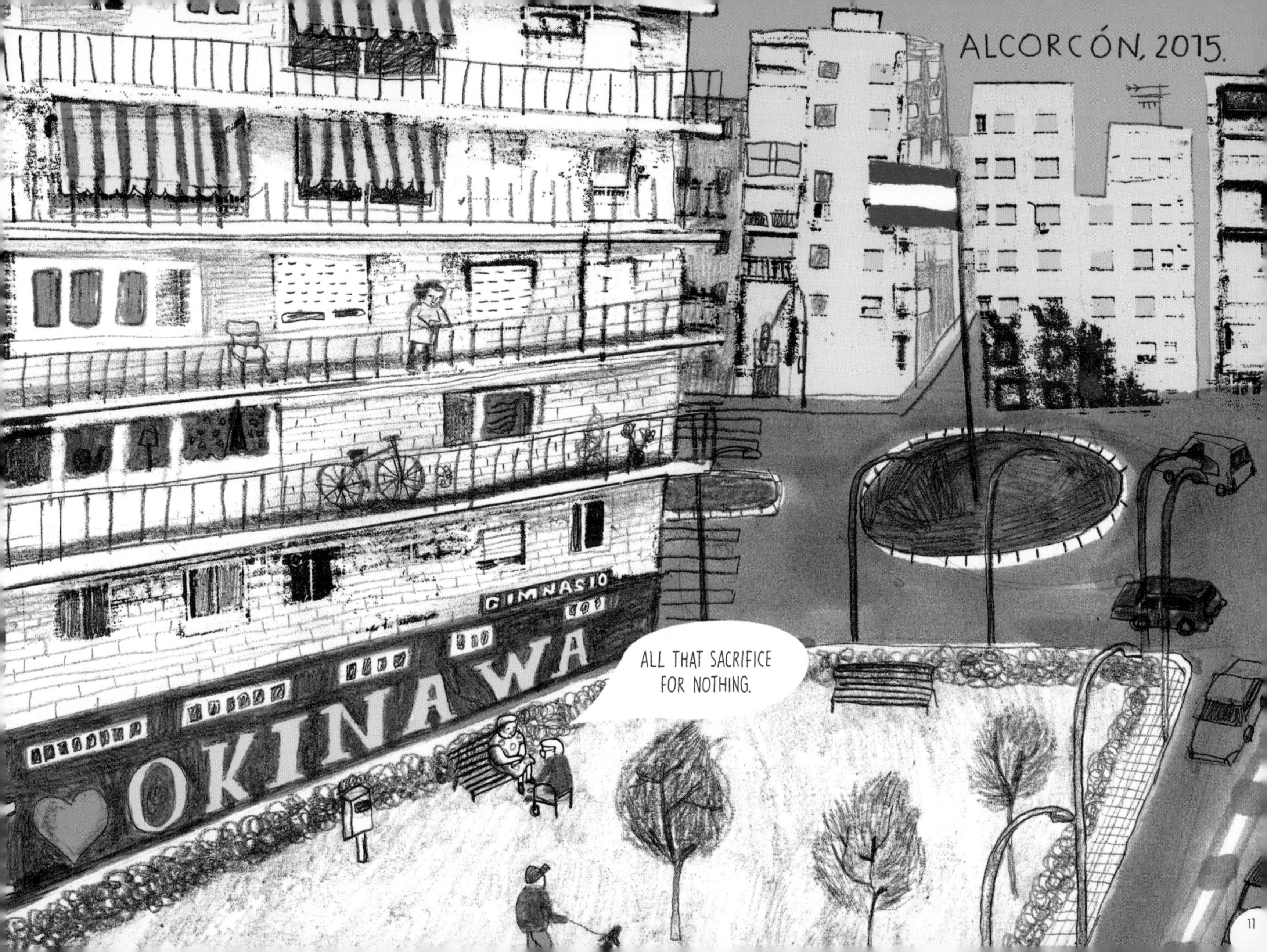
ALCORCÓN, 2015.
GIMNASIO
OKINAWA
ALL THAT SACRIFICE FOR NOTHING.

"I HATED THE BAR . . . . I HAD TO WAIT FOR MY AUNT, WHO WOULD GET OFF AT MIDNIGHT."

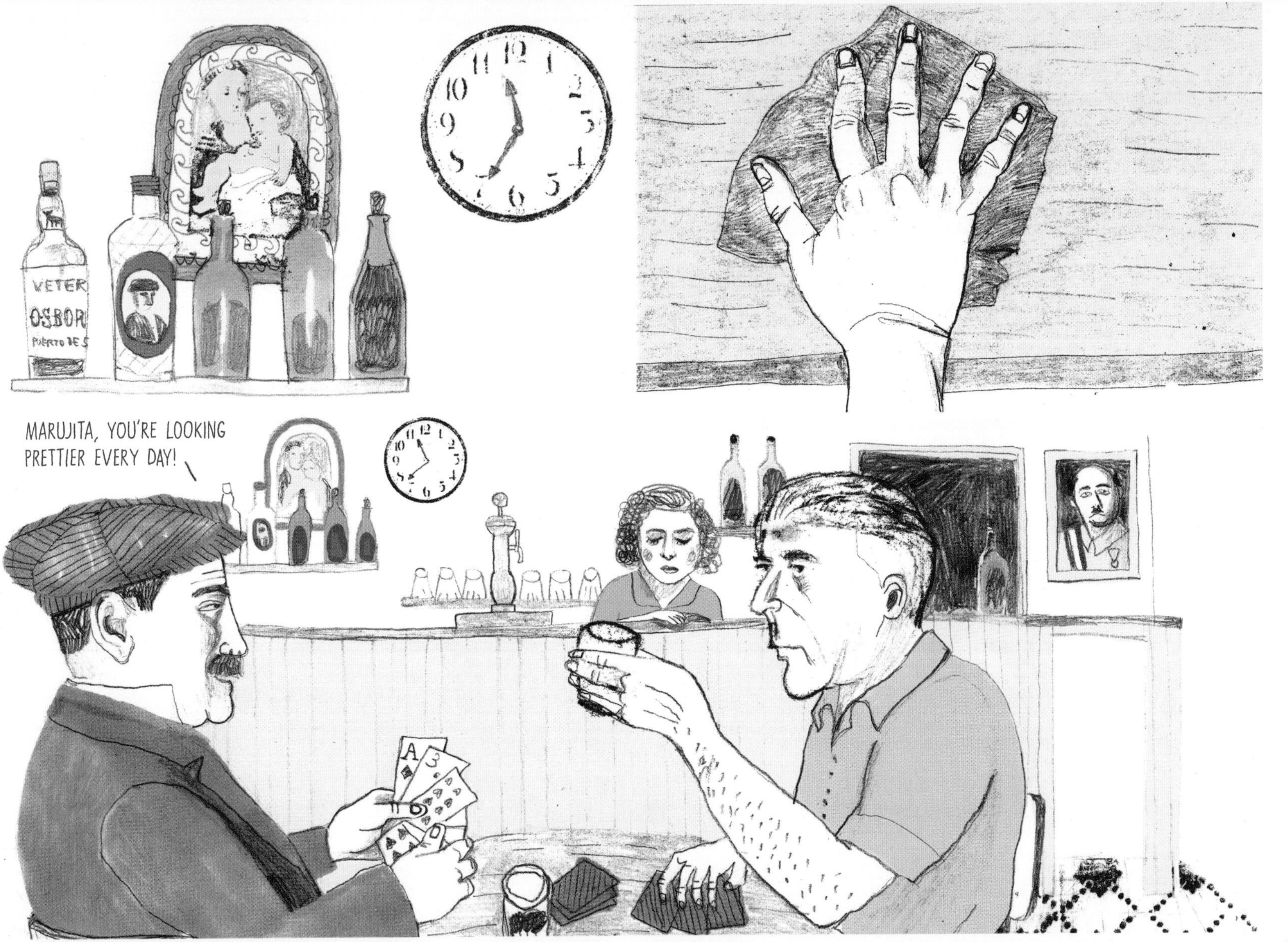
VETER
OSBOR
PUERTO DE S
MARUJITA, YOU'RE LOOKING PRETTIER EVERY DAY!

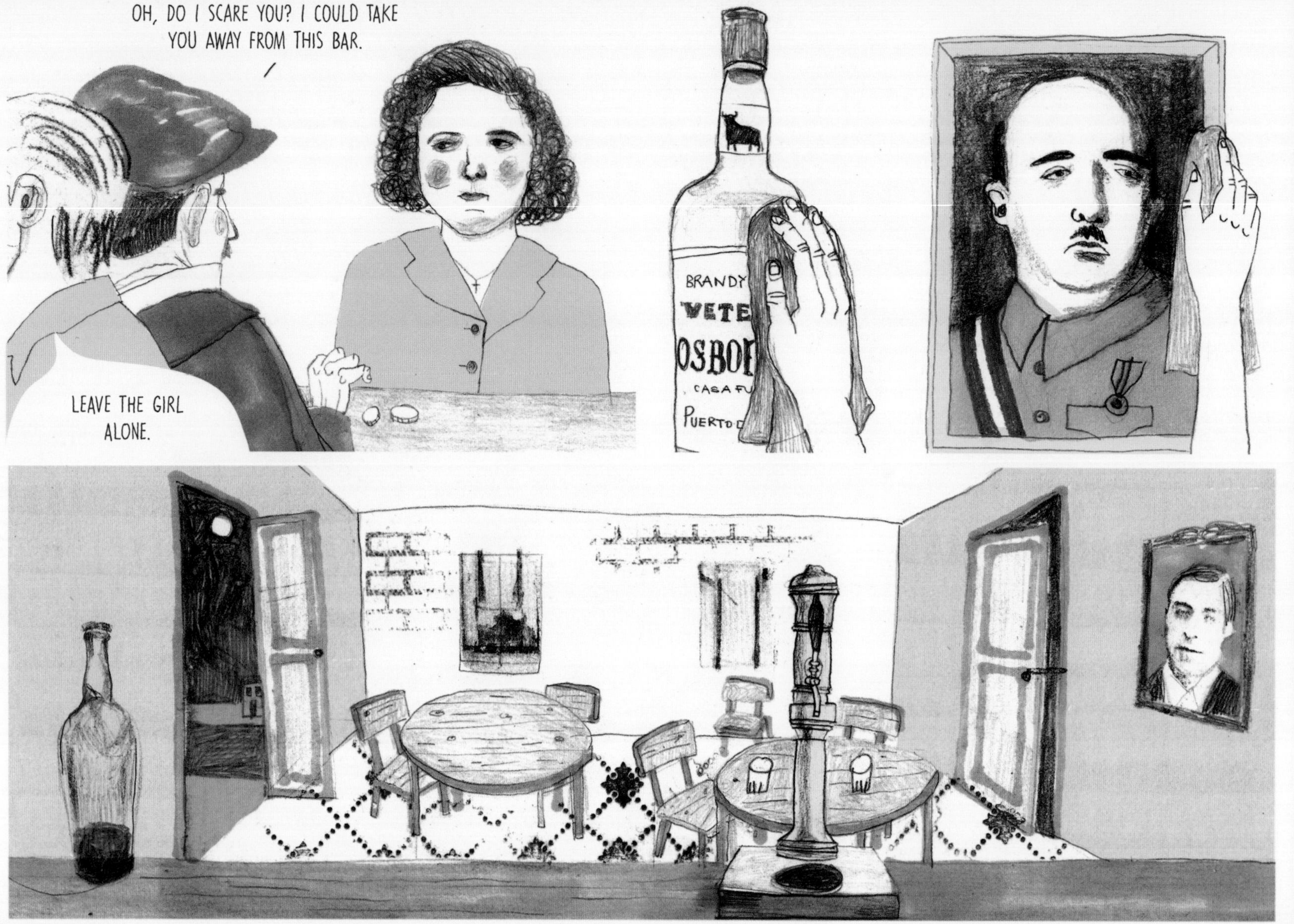
OH, DO I SCARE YOU? I COULD TAKE YOU AWAY FROM THIS BAR.
LEAVE THE GIRL ALONE.
BRANDY
VETE
OSBOR
CASA FU
PUERTO

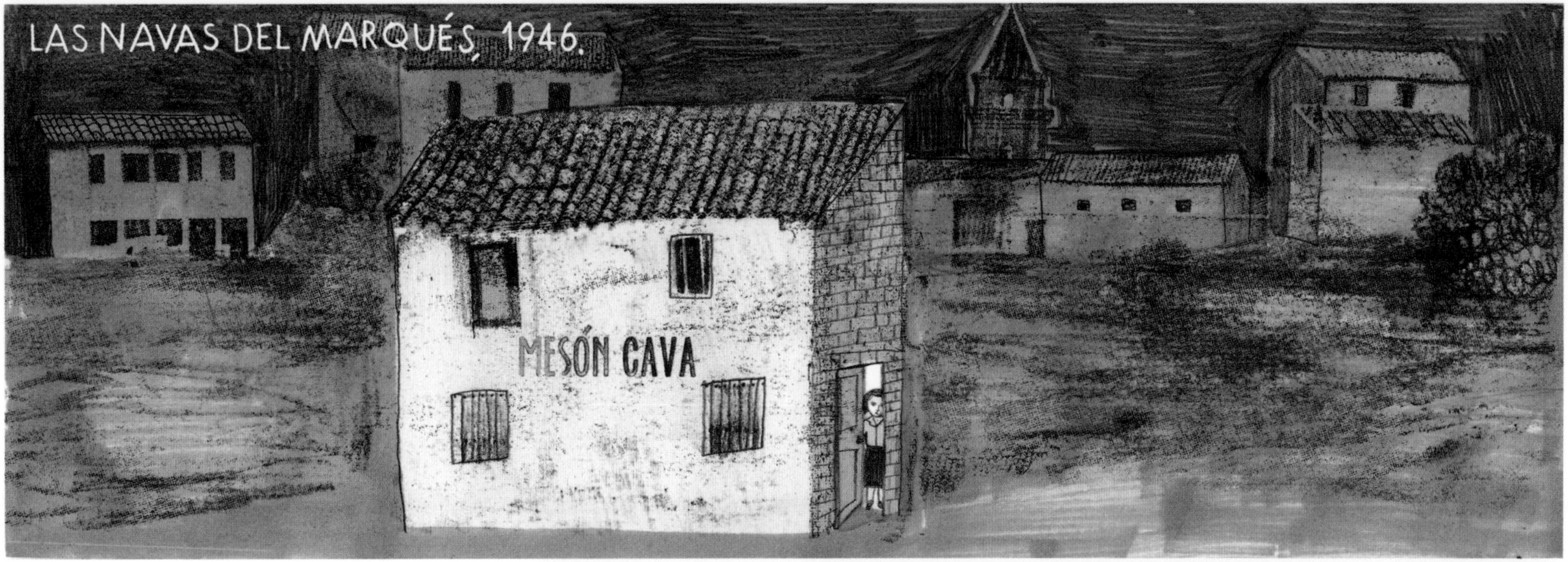
LAS NAVAS DEL MARQUÉS, 1946.
MESÓN CAVA

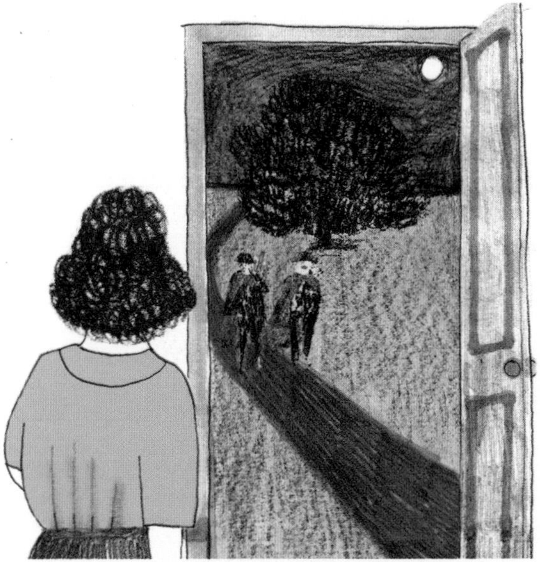

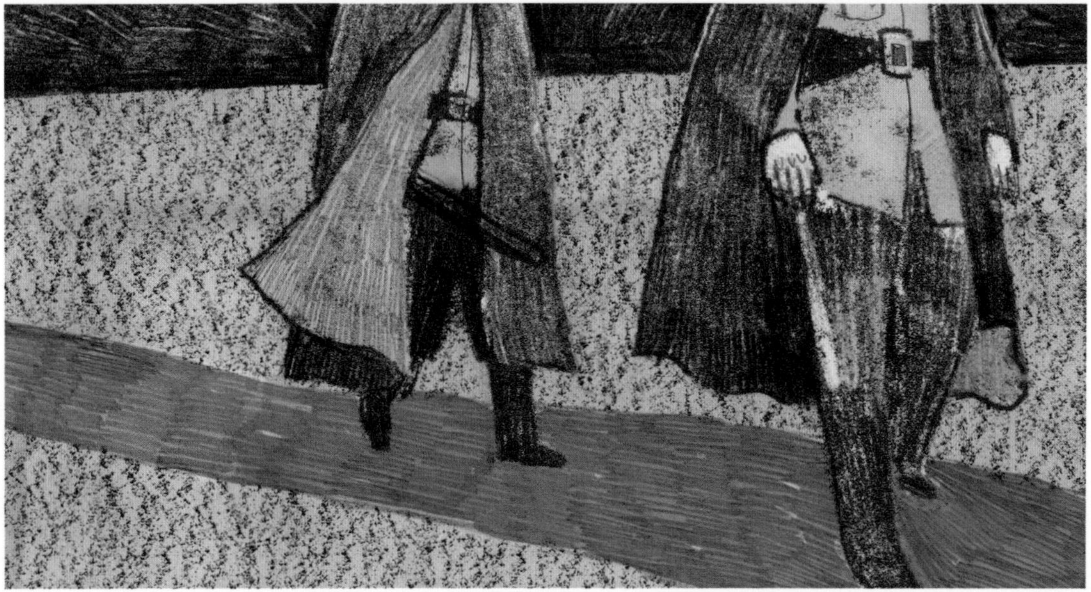

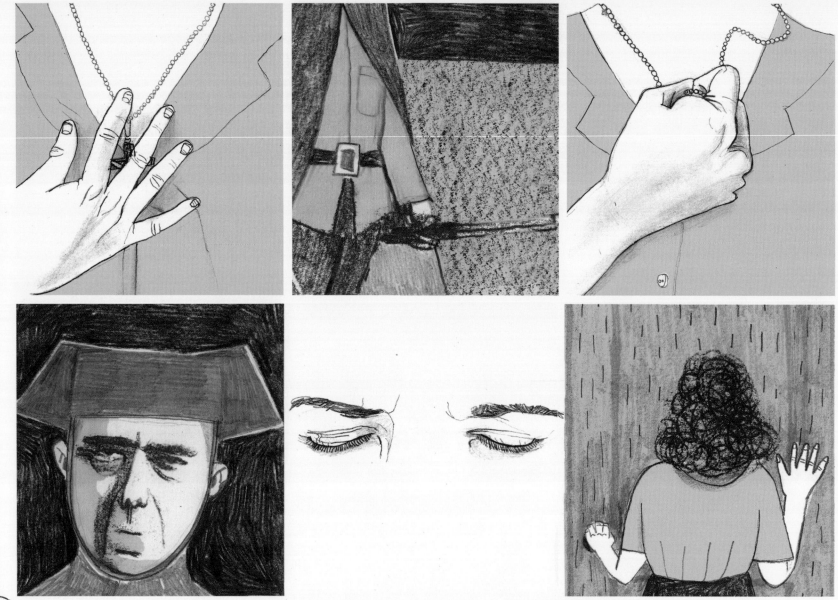

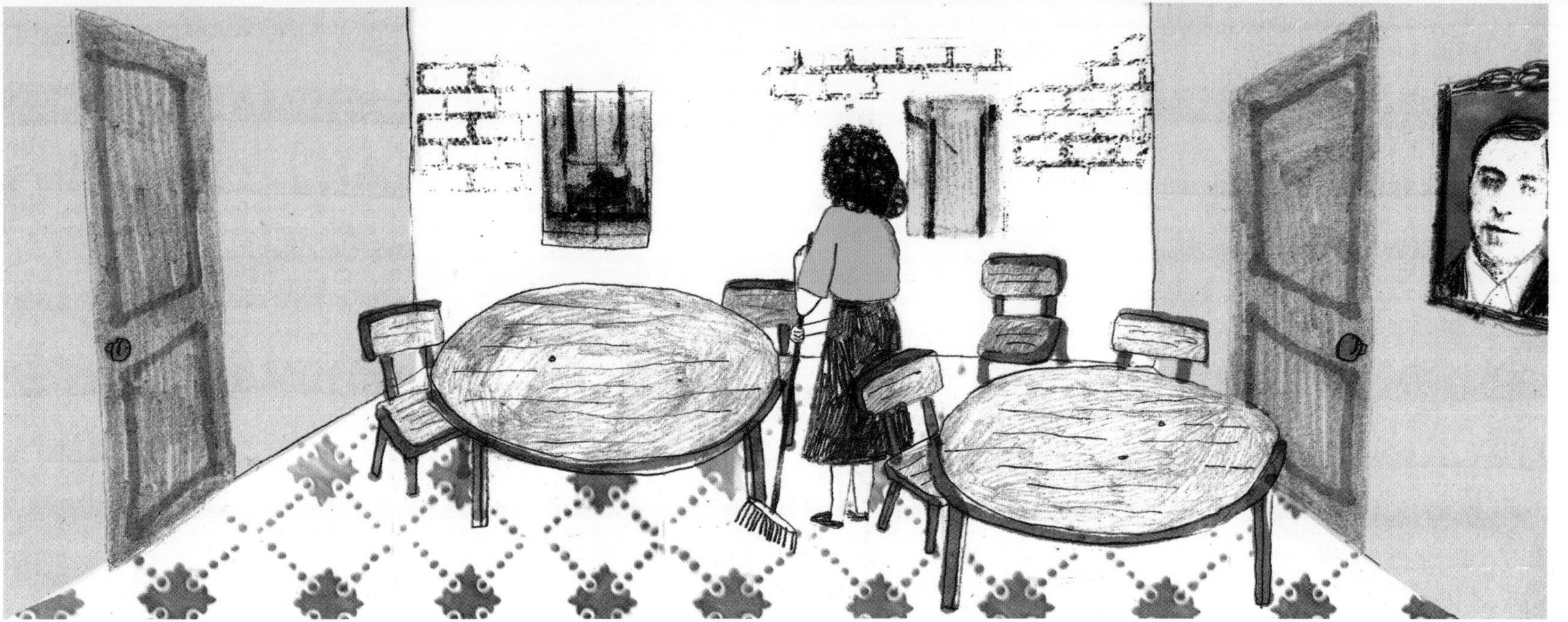

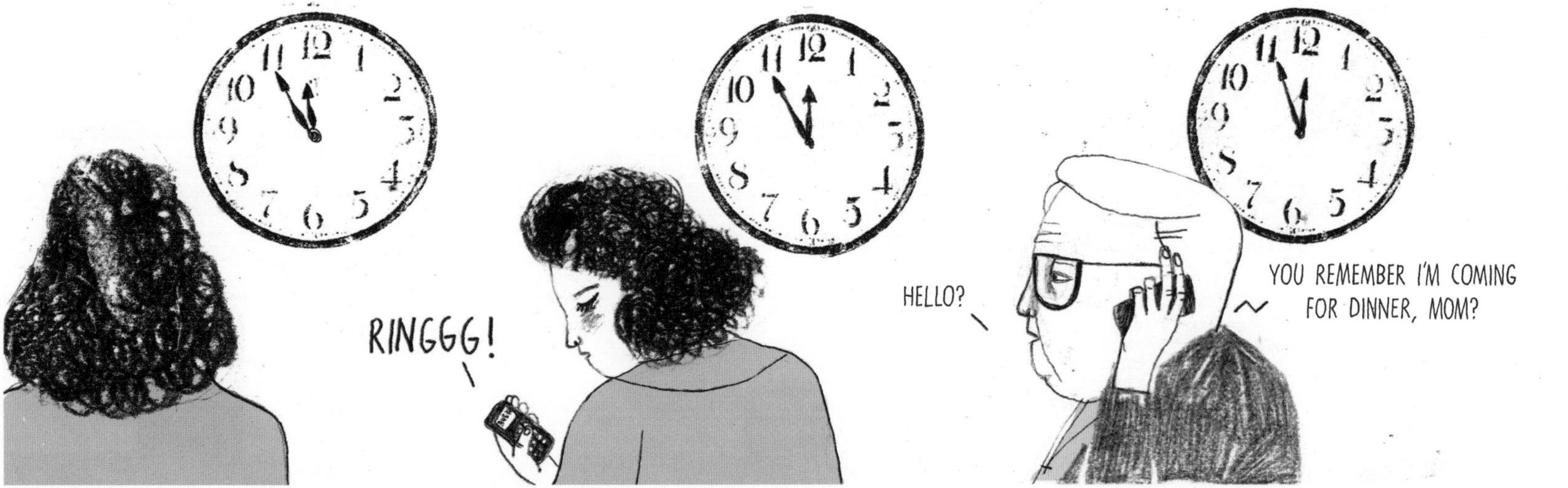
RINGGG!
HELLO?
YOU REMEMBER I'M COMING FOR DINNER, MOM?

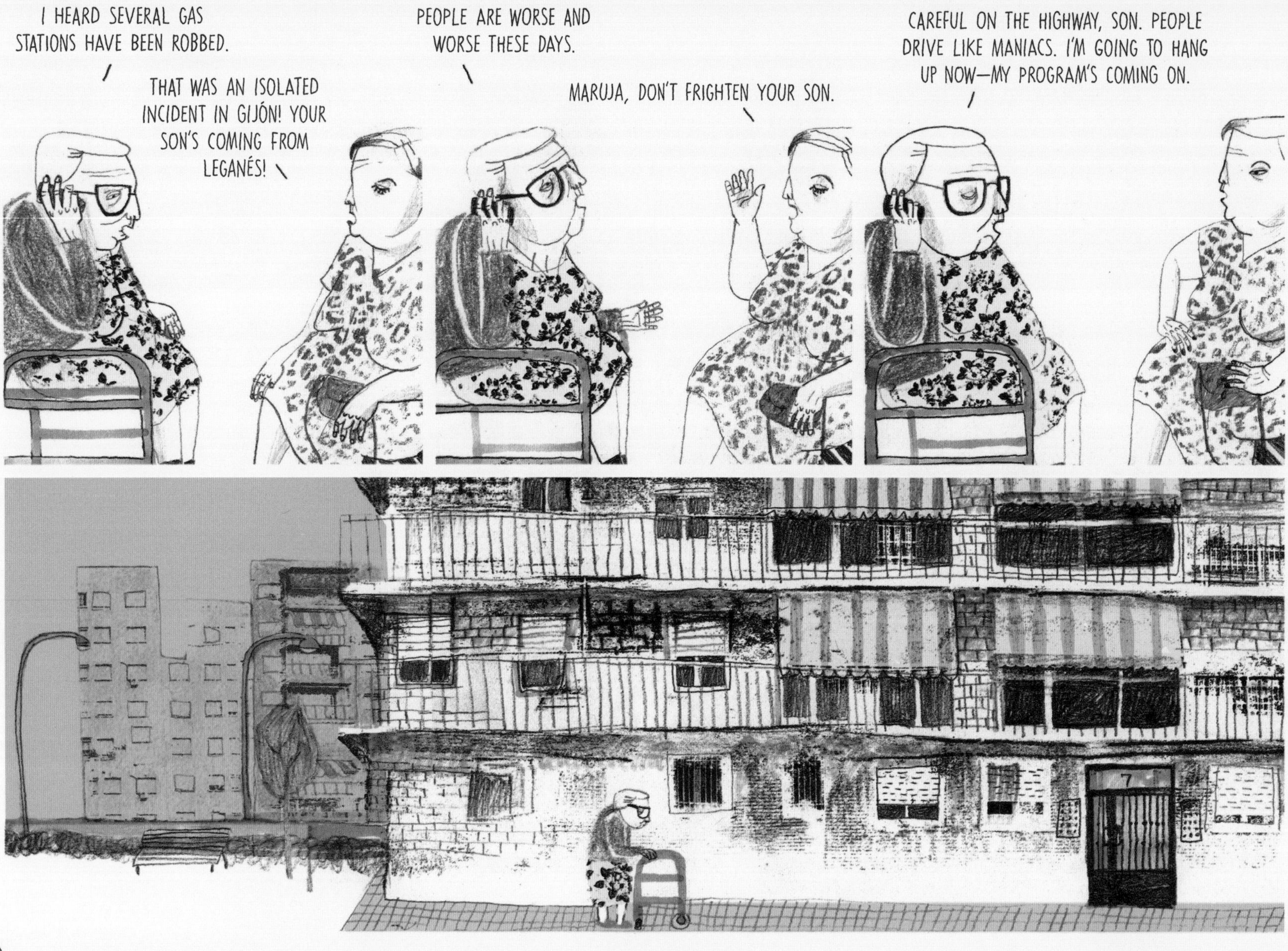
I HEARD SEVERAL GAS STATIONS HAVE BEEN ROBBED.
THAT WAS AN ISOLATED INCIDENT IN GIJÓN! YOUR SON'S COMING FROM LEGANÉS!
PEOPLE ARE WORSE AND WORSE THESE DAYS.
MARUJA, DON'T FRIGHTEN YOUR SON.
CAREFUL ON THE HIGHWAY, SON. PEOPLE DRIVE LIKE MANIACS. I'M GOING TO HANG UP NOW—MY PROGRAM'S COMING ON.
7

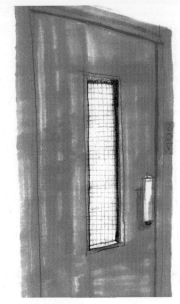

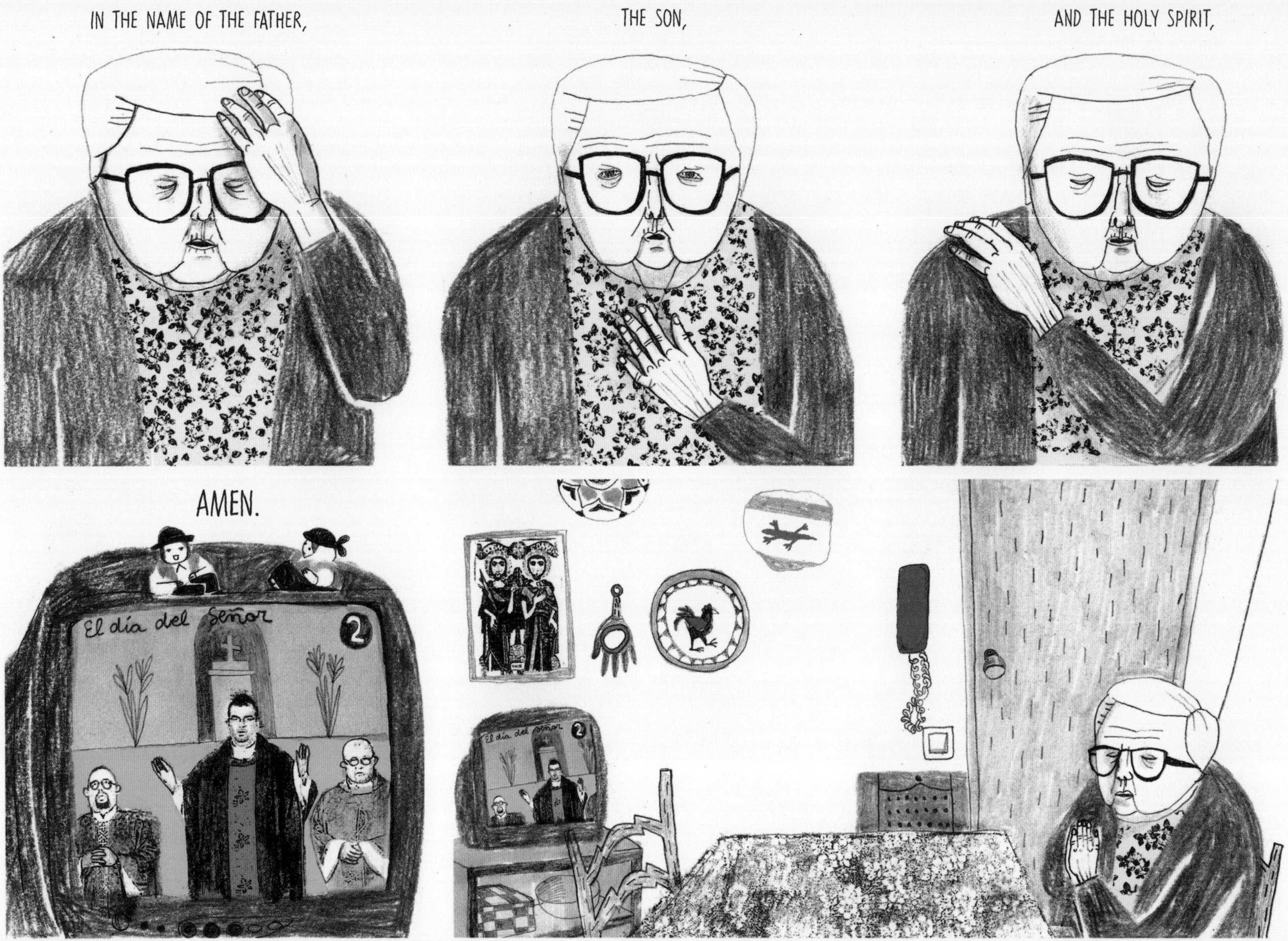
IN THE NAME OF THE FATHER,
THE SON,
AND THE HOLY SPIRIT,
AMEN.
El día del Señor
2

"MY FAMILY MANAGED TO MARRY
ME OFF . . . I DIDN'T WANT TO
AT FIRST. HE WAS MUCH OLDER
THAN ME. BUT IN THE END I
THOUGHT . . . LOOK, I'LL MARRY
THE DOCTOR AND THAT WAY I'LL
ESCAPE THE BAR."

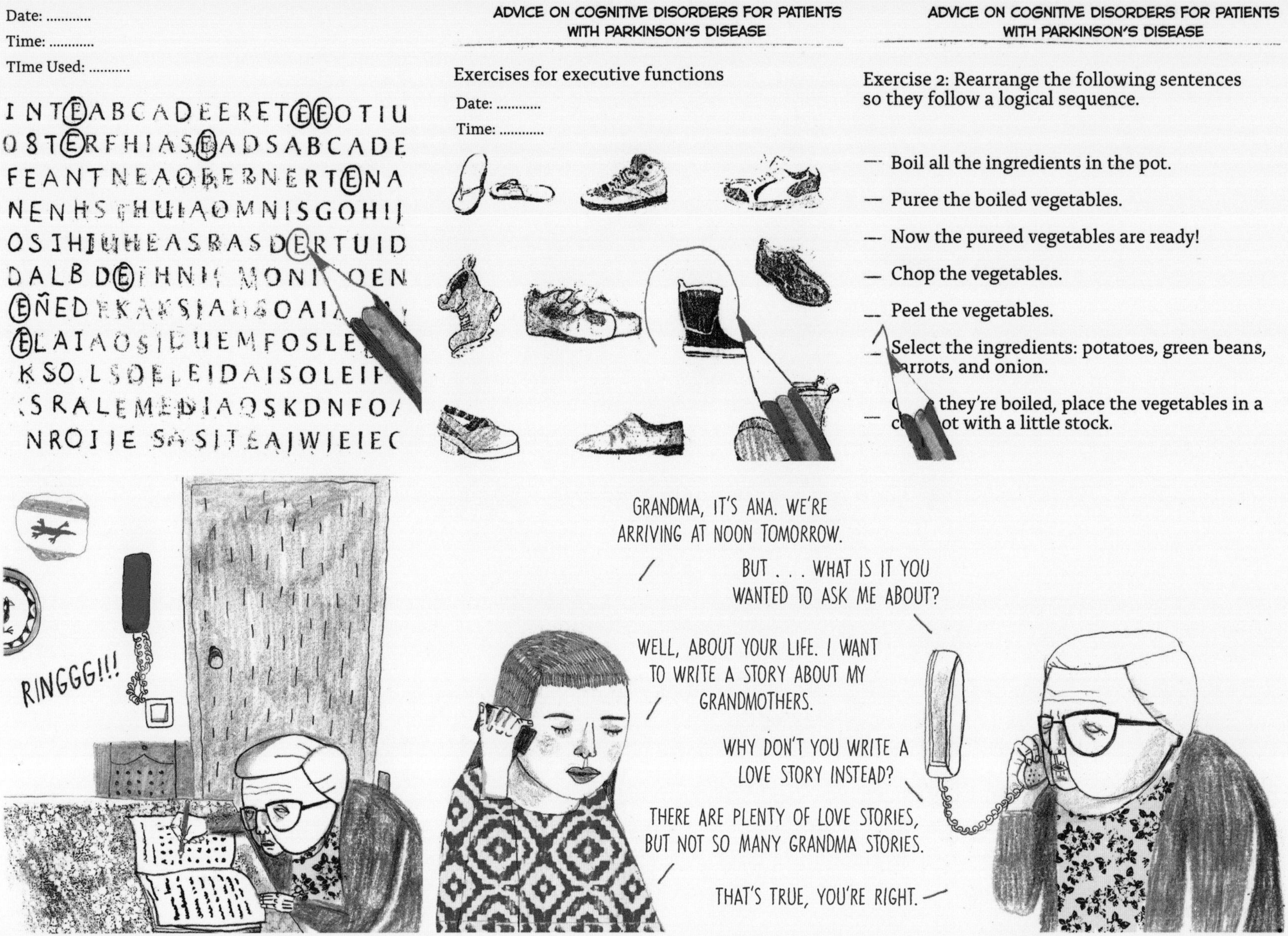

Date: ....
Time: ....
TIme Used: ....
ADVICE ON COGNITIVE DISORDERS FOR PATIENTS WITH PARKINSON'S DISEASE
Exercises for executive functions
Date: ....
Time: ....
ADVICE ON COGNITIVE DISORDERS FOR PATIENTS WITH PARKINSON'S DISEASE
Exercise 2: Rearrange the following sentences so they follow a logical sequence.
— Boil all the ingredients in the pot.
— Puree the boiled vegetables.
— Now the pureed vegetables are ready!
— Chop the vegetables.
— Peel the vegetables.
— Select the ingredients: potatoes, green beans, arrots, and onion.
they're boiled, place the vegetables in a ot with a little stock.
RINGGG!!!
GRANDMA, IT'S ANA. WE'RE ARRIVING AT NOON TOMORROW.
BUT . . . WHAT IS IT YOU WANTED TO ASK ME ABOUT?
WELL, ABOUT YOUR LIFE. I WANT TO WRITE A STORY ABOUT MY GRANDMOTHERS.
WHY DON'T YOU WRITE A LOVE STORY INSTEAD?
THERE ARE PLENTY OF LOVE STORIES, BUT NOT SO MANY GRANDMA STORIES.
THAT'S TRUE, YOU'RE RIGHT.

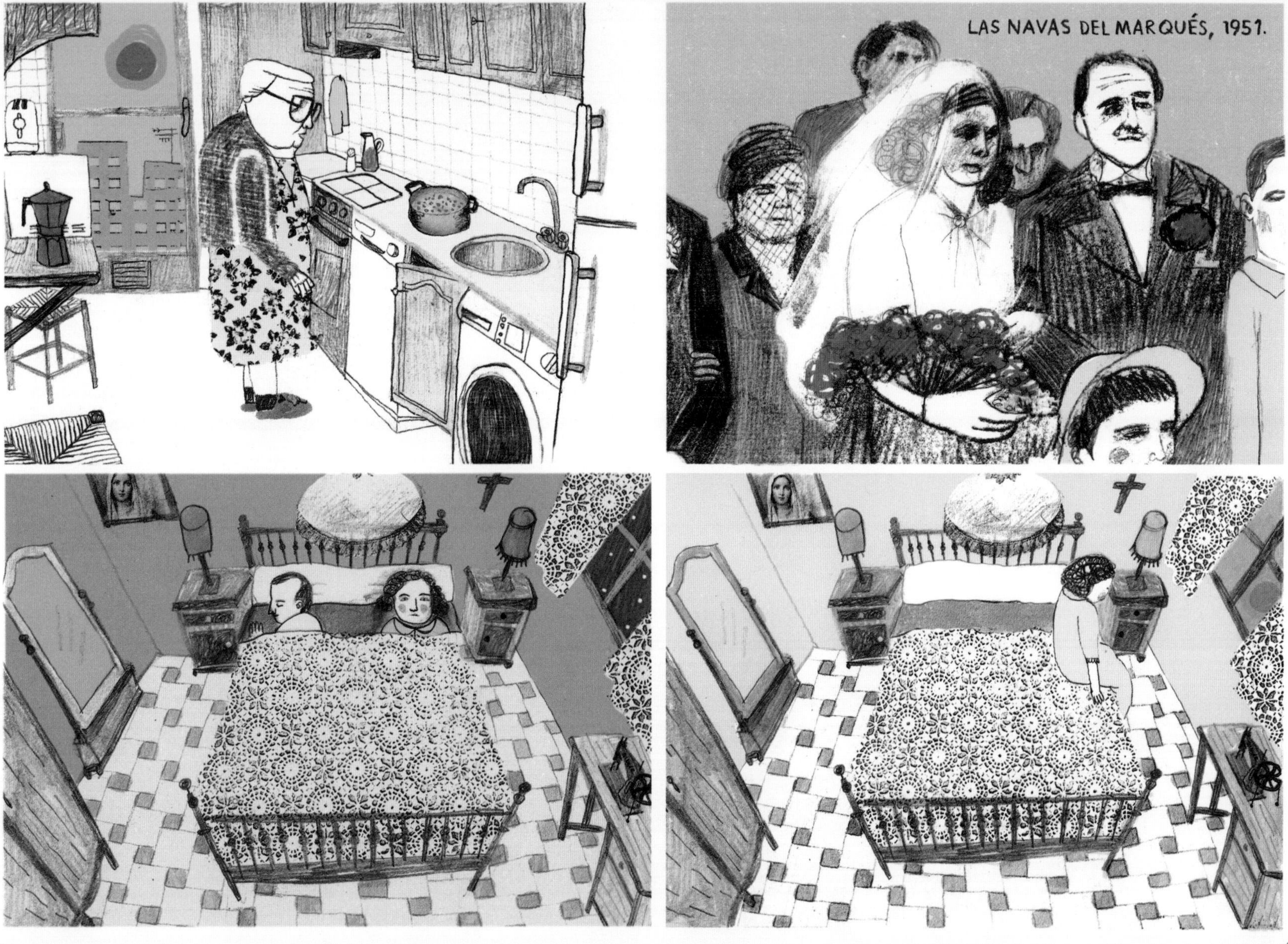
LAS NAVAS DEL MARQUÉS, 1951.

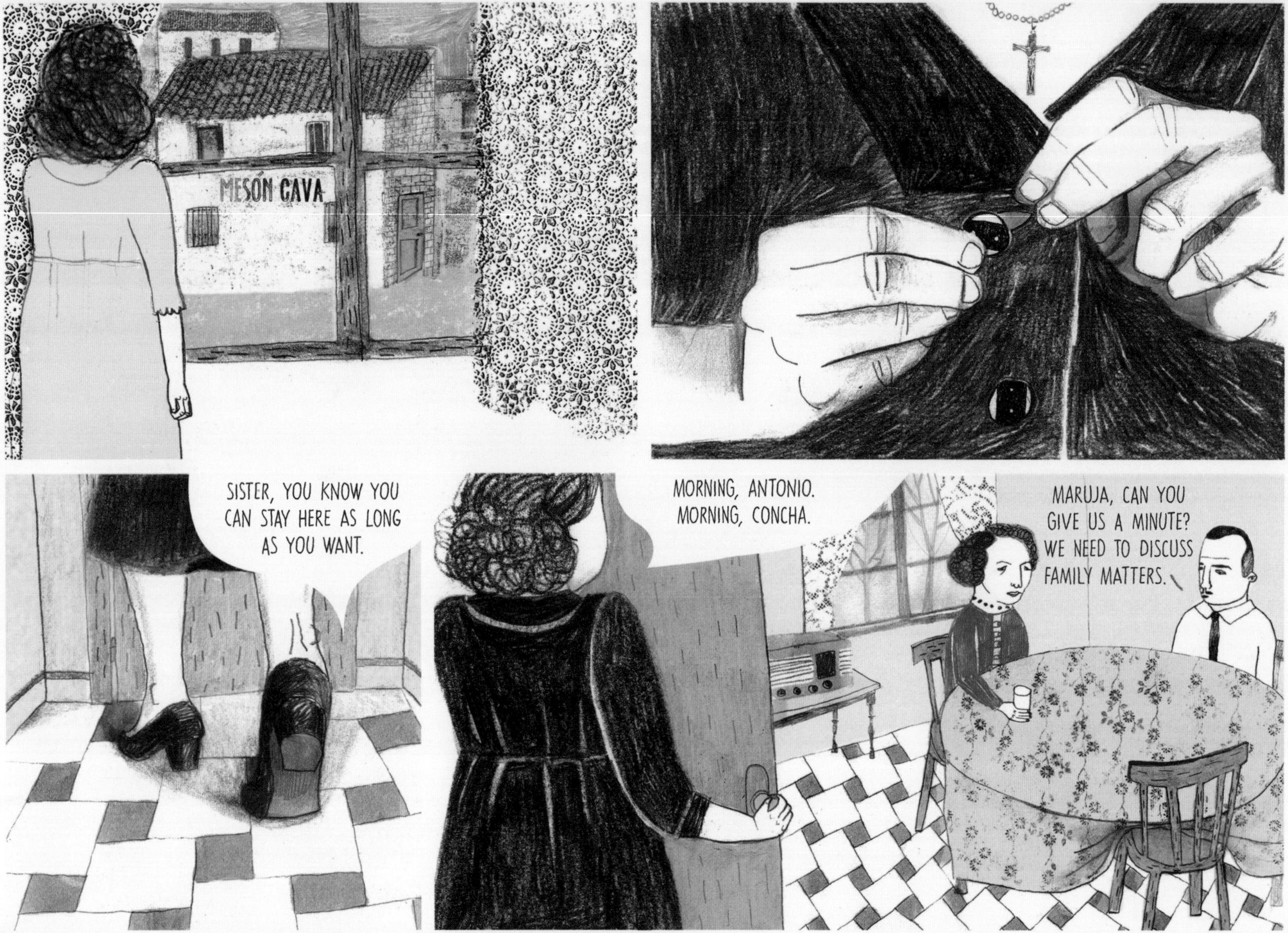
MESÓN CAVA
SISTER, YOU KNOW YOU CAN STAY HERE AS LONG AS YOU WANT.
MORNING, ANTONIO. MORNING, CONCHA.
MARUJA, CAN YOU GIVE US A MINUTE? WE NEED TO DISCUSS FAMILY MATTERS.

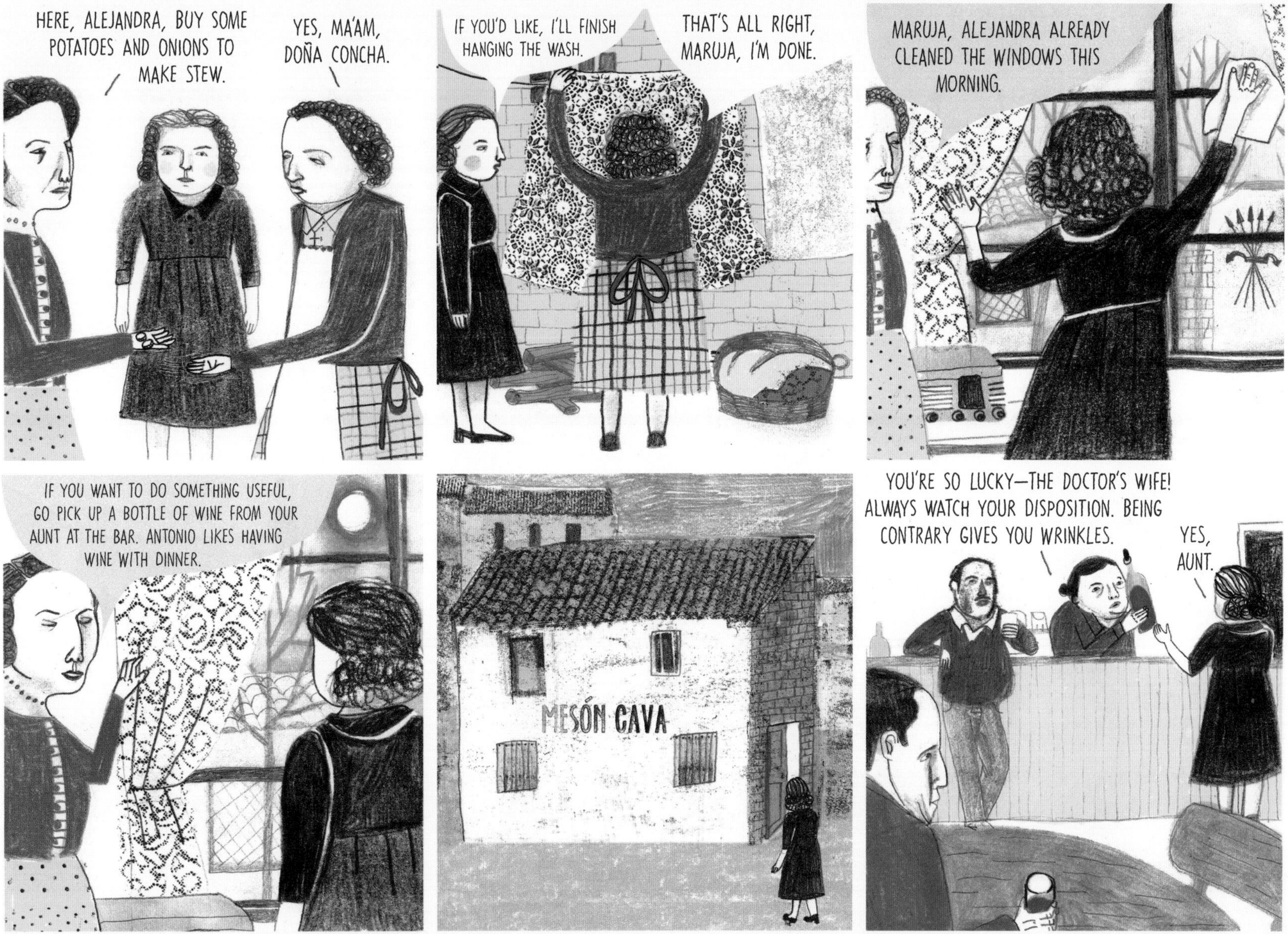
HERE, ALEJANDRA, BUY SOME POTATOES AND ONIONS TO MAKE STEW.
YES, MA'AM, DOÑA CONCHA.
IF YOU'D LIKE, I'LL FINISH HANGING THE WASH.
THAT'S ALL RIGHT, MARUJA, I'M DONE.
MARUJA, ALEJANDRA ALREADY CLEANED THE WINDOWS THIS MORNING.
IF YOU WANT TO DO SOMETHING USEFUL, GO PICK UP A BOTTLE OF WINE FROM YOUR AUNT AT THE BAR. ANTONIO LIKES HAVING WINE WITH DINNER.
MESÓN CAVA
YOU'RE SO LUCKY—THE DOCTOR'S WIFE! ALWAYS WATCH YOUR DISPOSITION. BEING CONTRARY GIVES YOU WRINKLES.
YES, AUNT.

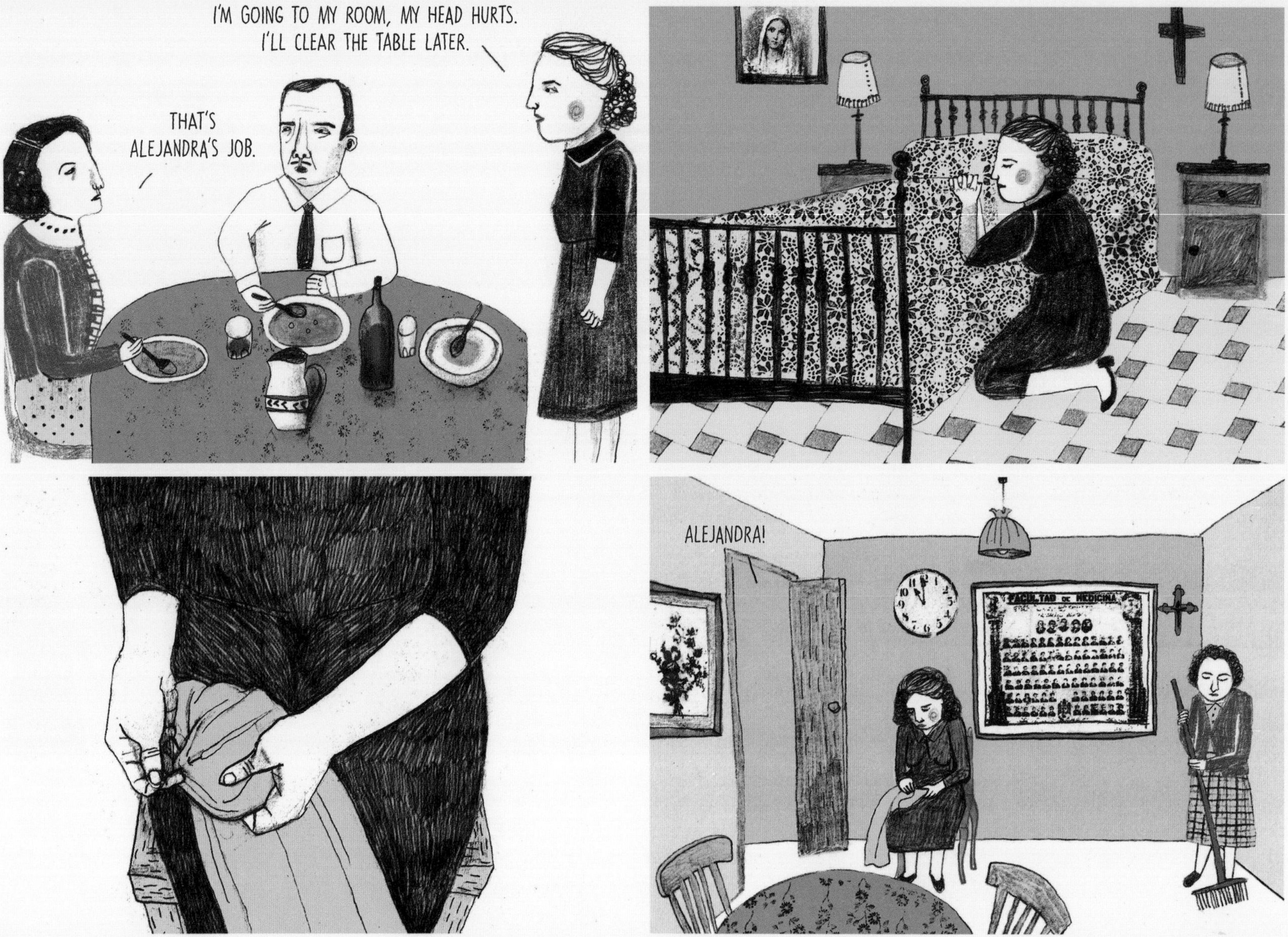
I'M GOING TO MY ROOM, MY HEAD HURTS. I'LL CLEAR THE TABLE LATER.
THAT'S ALEJANDRA'S JOB.
ALEJANDRA!
FACULTAD DE MEDICINA

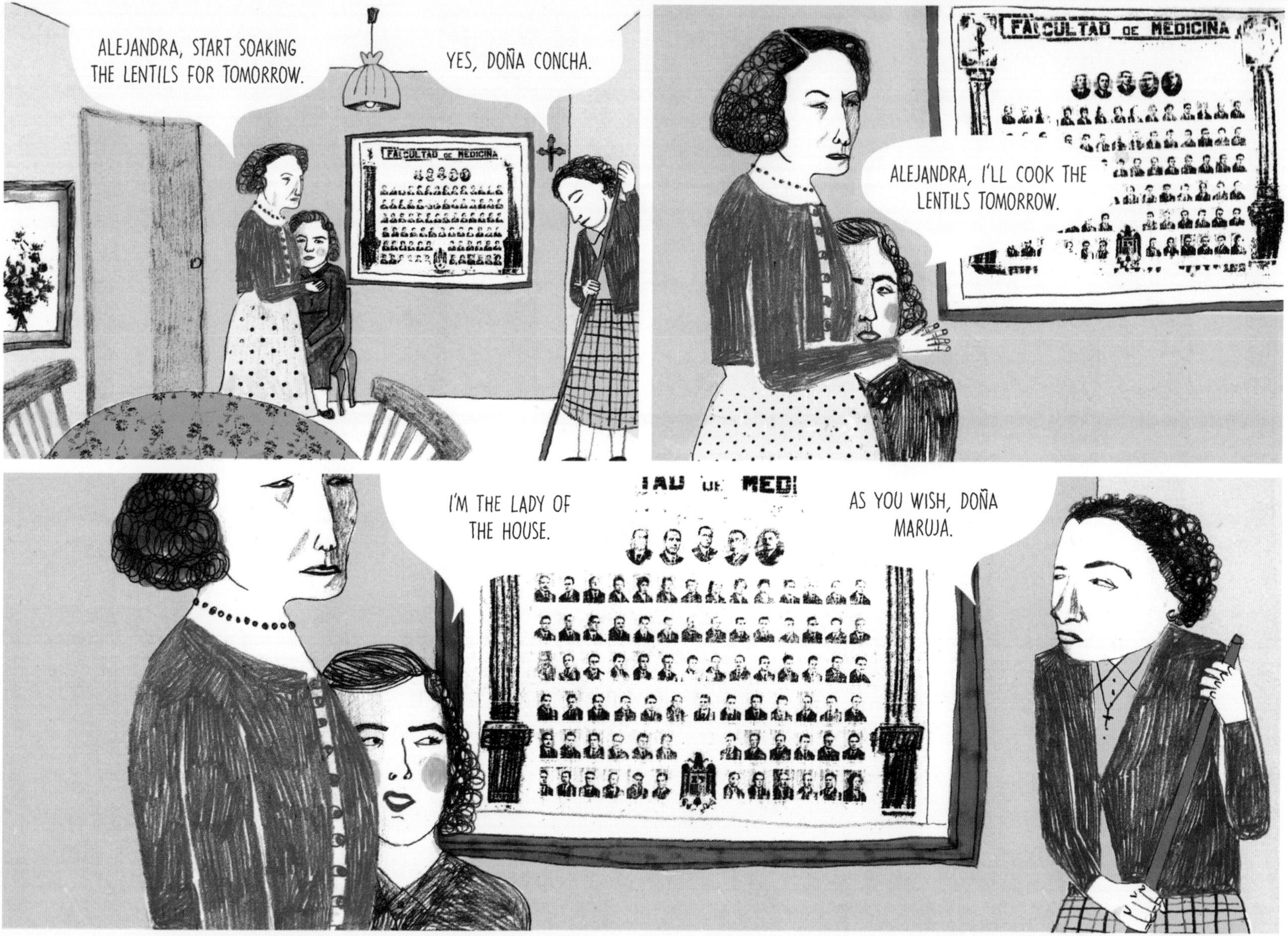
ALEJANDRA, START SOAKING THE LENTILS FOR TOMORROW.
YES, DOÑA CONCHA.
FACULTAD DE MEDICINA
ALEJANDRA, I'LL COOK THE LENTILS TOMORROW.
I'M THE LADY OF THE HOUSE.
AS YOU WISH, DOÑA MARUJA.

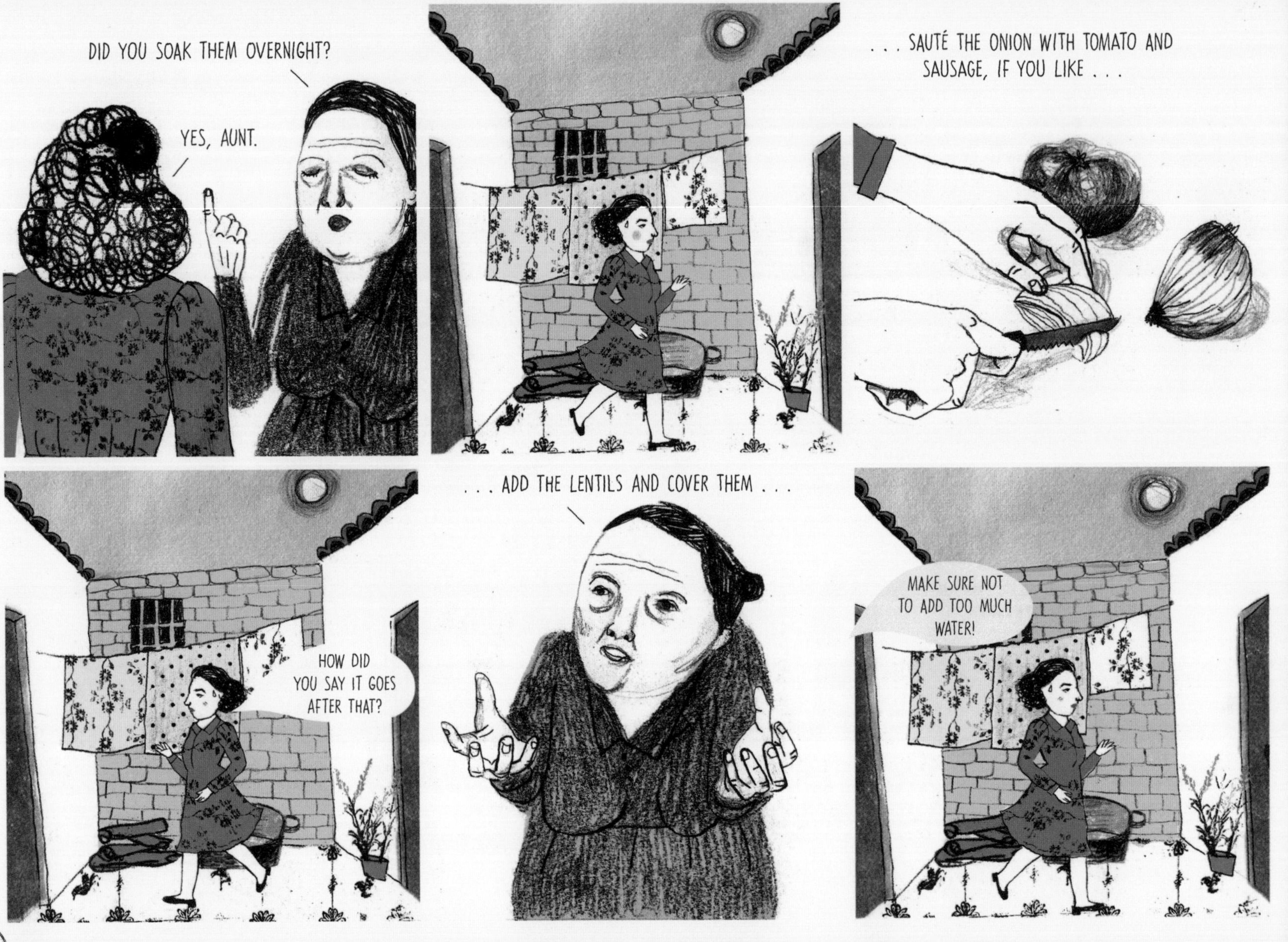
DID YOU SOAK THEM OVERNIGHT?
YES, AUNT.
. . . SAUTÉ THE ONION WITH TOMATO AND SAUSAGE, IF YOU LIKE . . .
HOW DID YOU SAY IT GOES AFTER THAT?
. . . ADD THE LENTILS AND COVER THEM . . .
MAKE SURE NOT TO ADD TOO MUCH WATER!

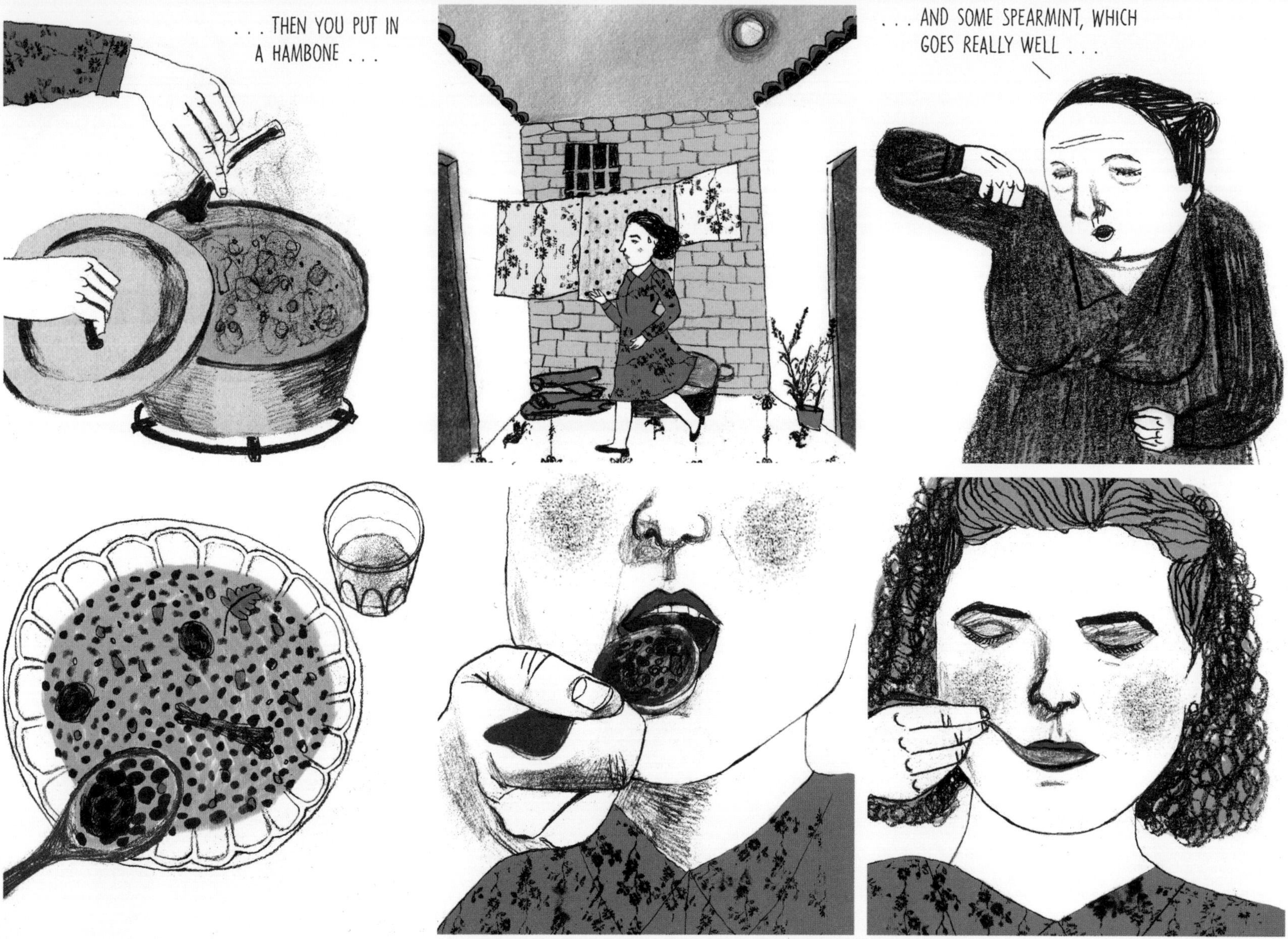
. . . THEN YOU PUT IN A HAMBONE . . .
. . . AND SOME SPEARMINT, WHICH GOES REALLY WELL . . .

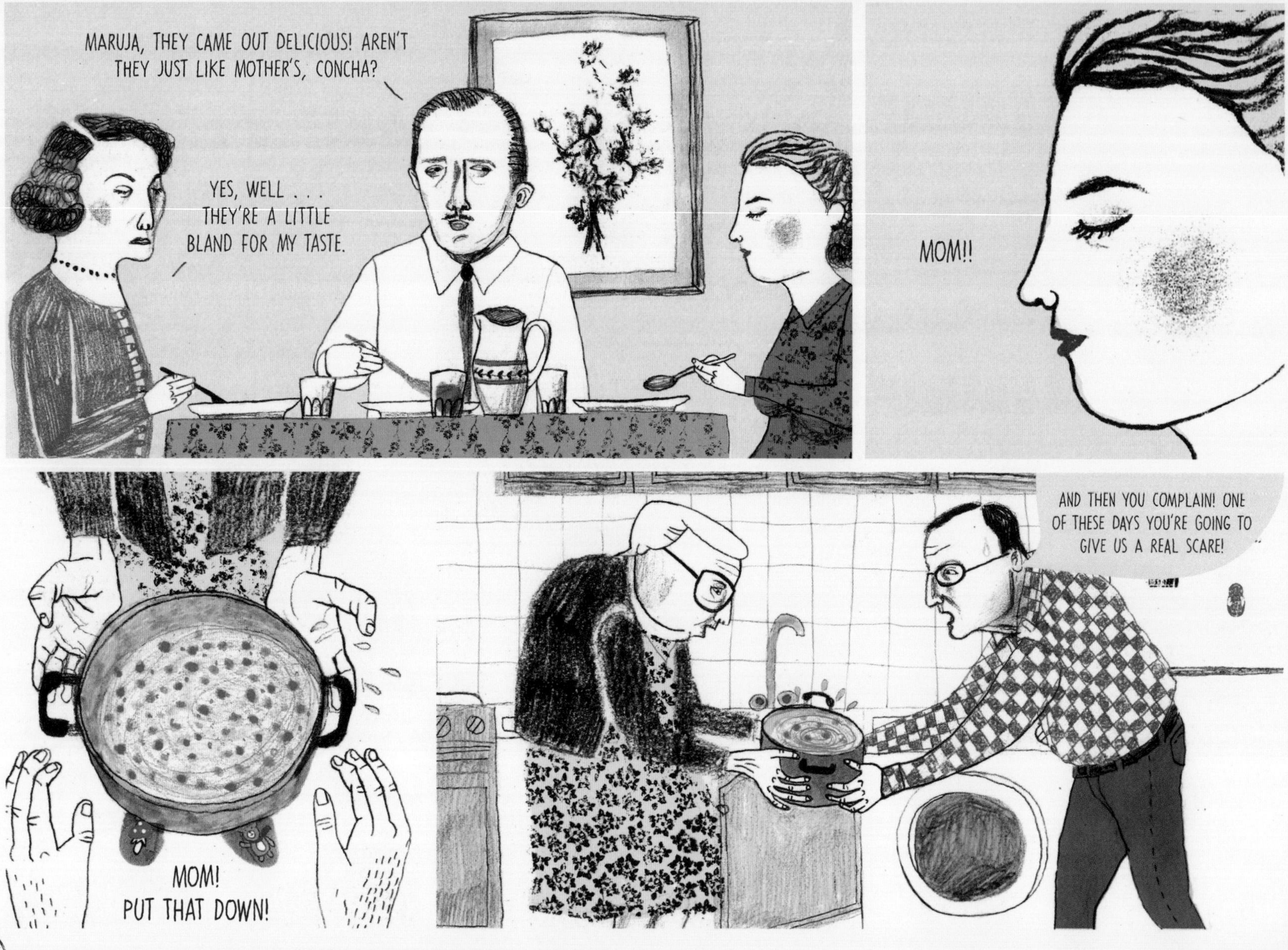
MARUJA, THEY CAME OUT DELICIOUS! AREN'T THEY JUST LIKE MOTHER'S, CONCHA?
YES, WELL . . . THEY'RE A LITTLE BLAND FOR MY TASTE.
MOM!!
MOM! PUT THAT DOWN!
AND THEN YOU COMPLAIN! ONE OF THESE DAYS YOU'RE GOING TO GIVE US A REAL SCARE!

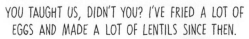

BUT YOU DON'T KNOW HOW!

YOU TAUGHT US, DIDN'T YOU? I'VE FRIED A LOT OF EGGS AND MADE A LOT OF LENTILS SINCE THEN.

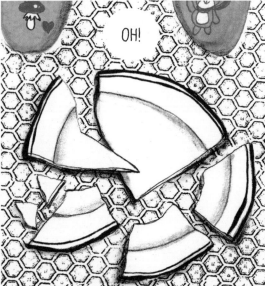

OH!

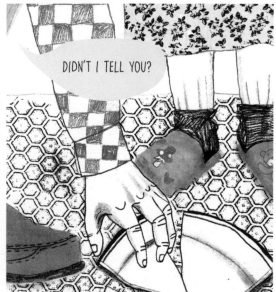

DIDN'T I TELL YOU?

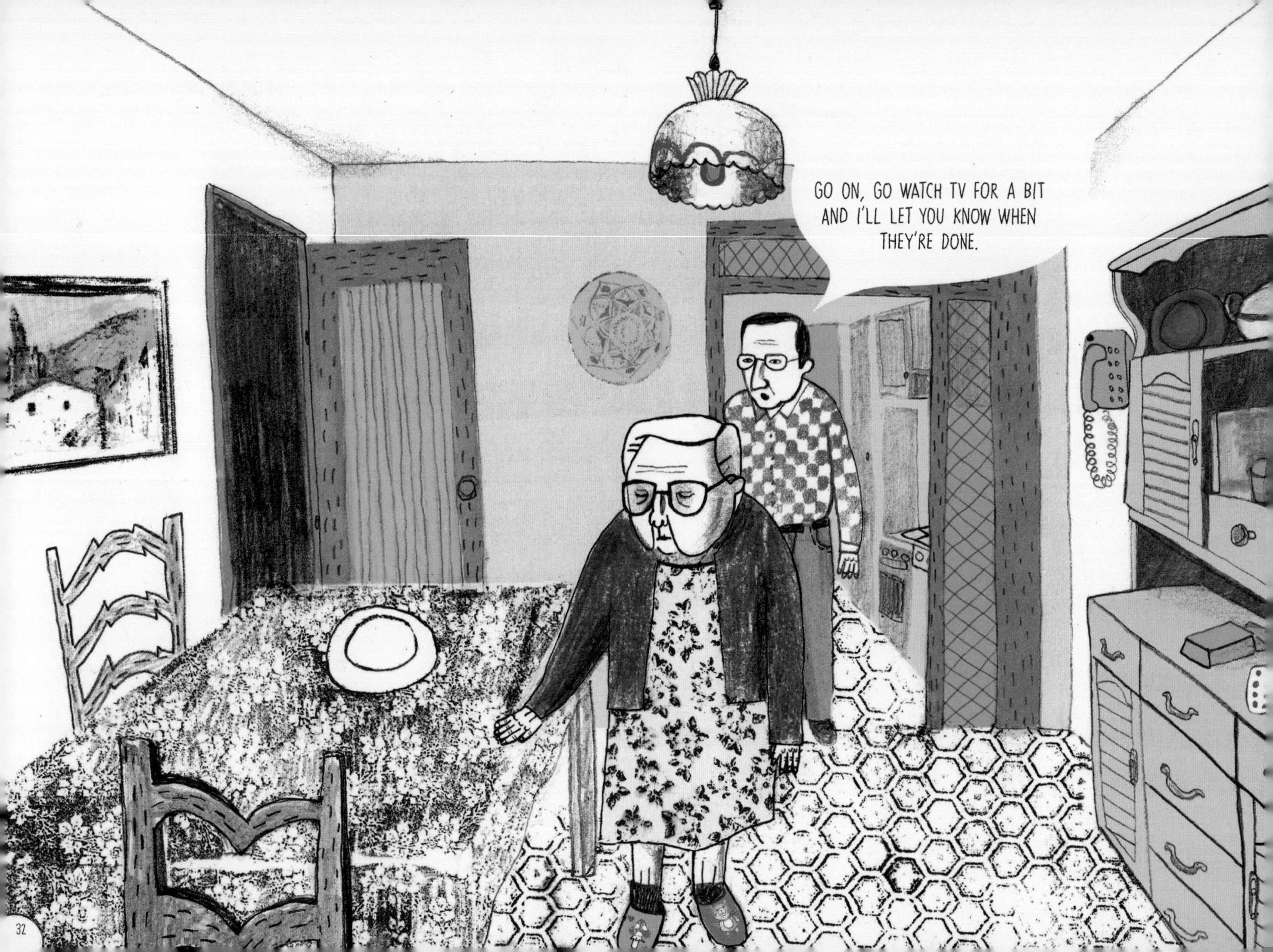
GO ON, GO WATCH TV FOR A BIT AND I'LL LET YOU KNOW WHEN THEY'RE DONE.

"I WENT UP TO A BALCONY WE HAD, AND AS I GAZED AT
THE RIVER, I REMEMBERED LAS NAVAS AND FELT SAD.
HE WAS A DOCTOR AND I WAS NOBODY."

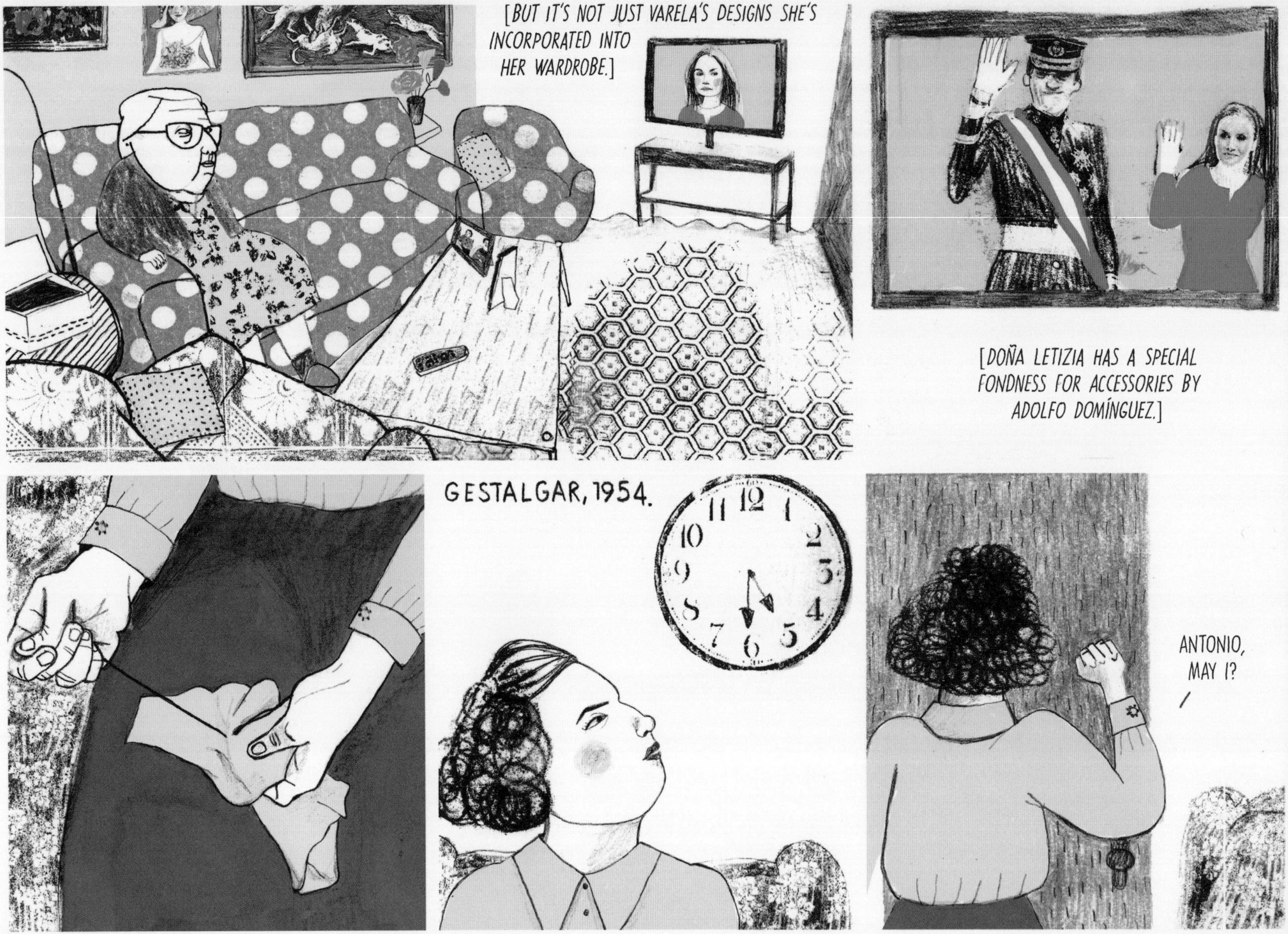
[BUT IT'S NOT JUST VARELA'S DESIGNS SHE'S INCORPORATED INTO HER WARDROBE.]
[DOÑA LETIZIA HAS A SPECIAL FONDNESS FOR ACCESSORIES BY ADOLFO DOMÍNGUEZ.]
GESTALGAR, 1954.
ANTONIO, MAY I?

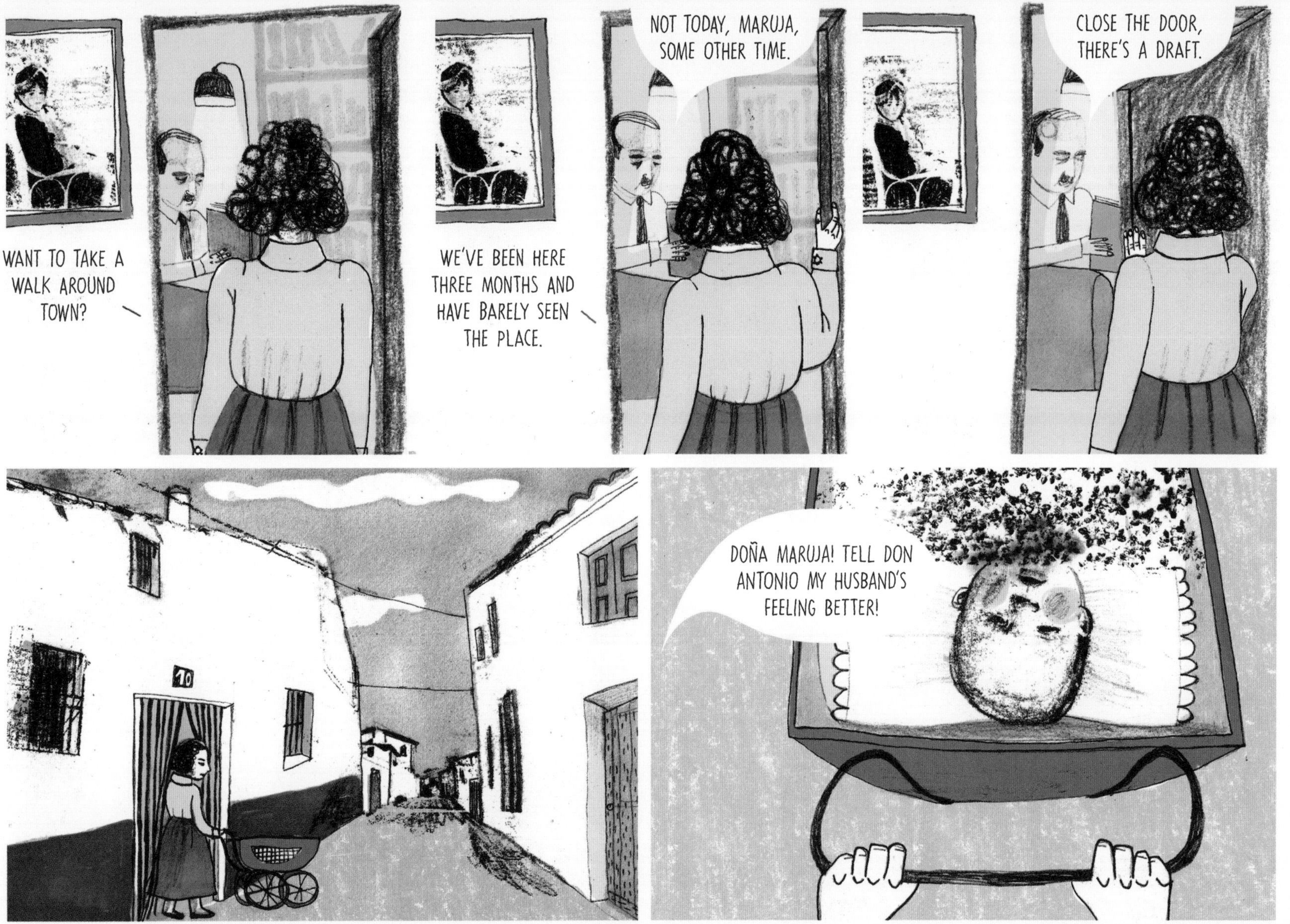

WANT TO TAKE A WALK AROUND TOWN?
WE'VE BEEN HERE THREE MONTHS AND HAVE BARELY SEEN THE PLACE.
NOT TODAY, MARUJA, SOME OTHER TIME.
CLOSE THE DOOR, THERE'S A DRAFT.
10
DOÑA MARUJA! TELL DON ANTONIO MY HUSBAND'S FEELING BETTER!

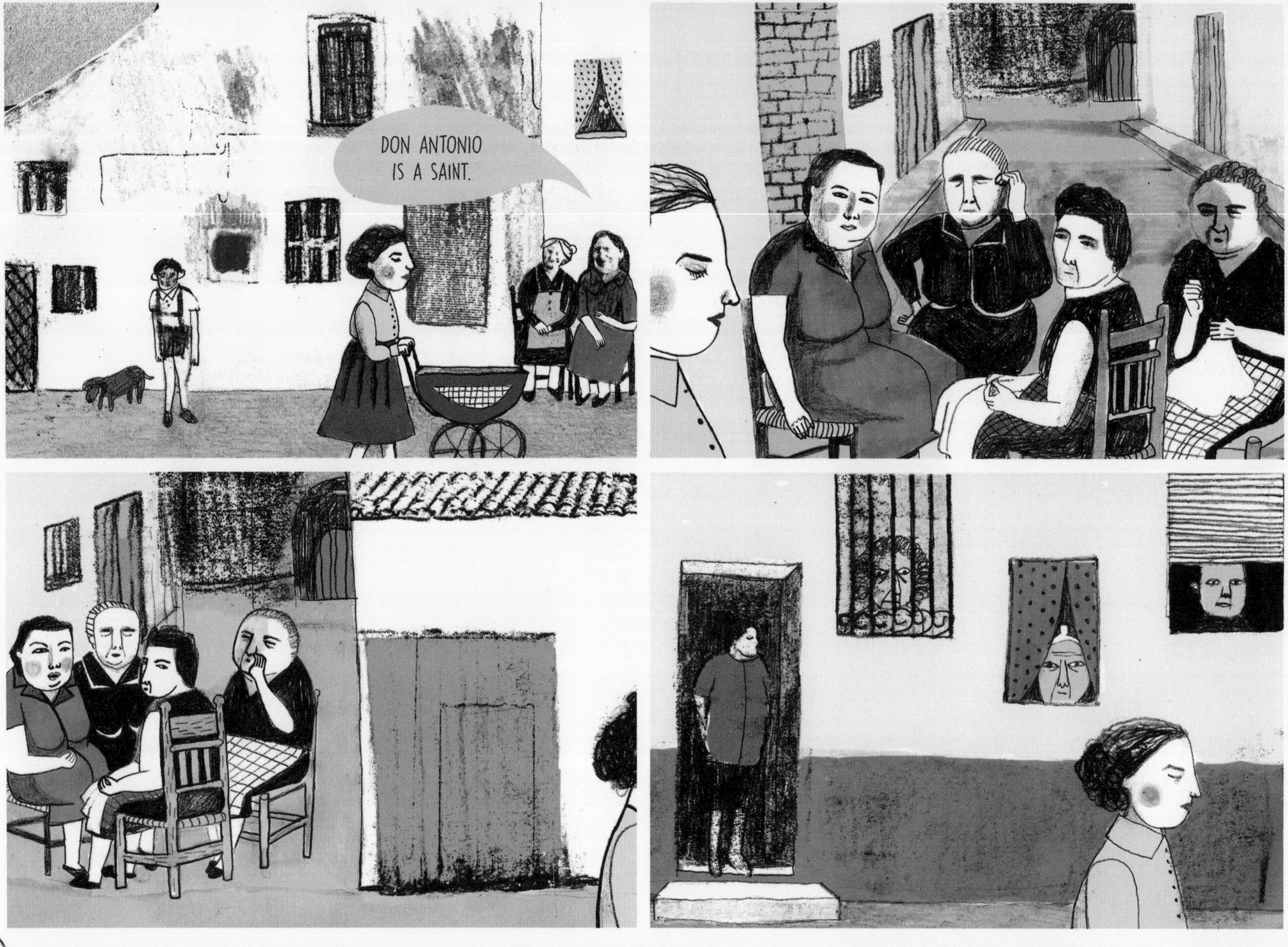
DON ANTONIO
IS A SAINT.

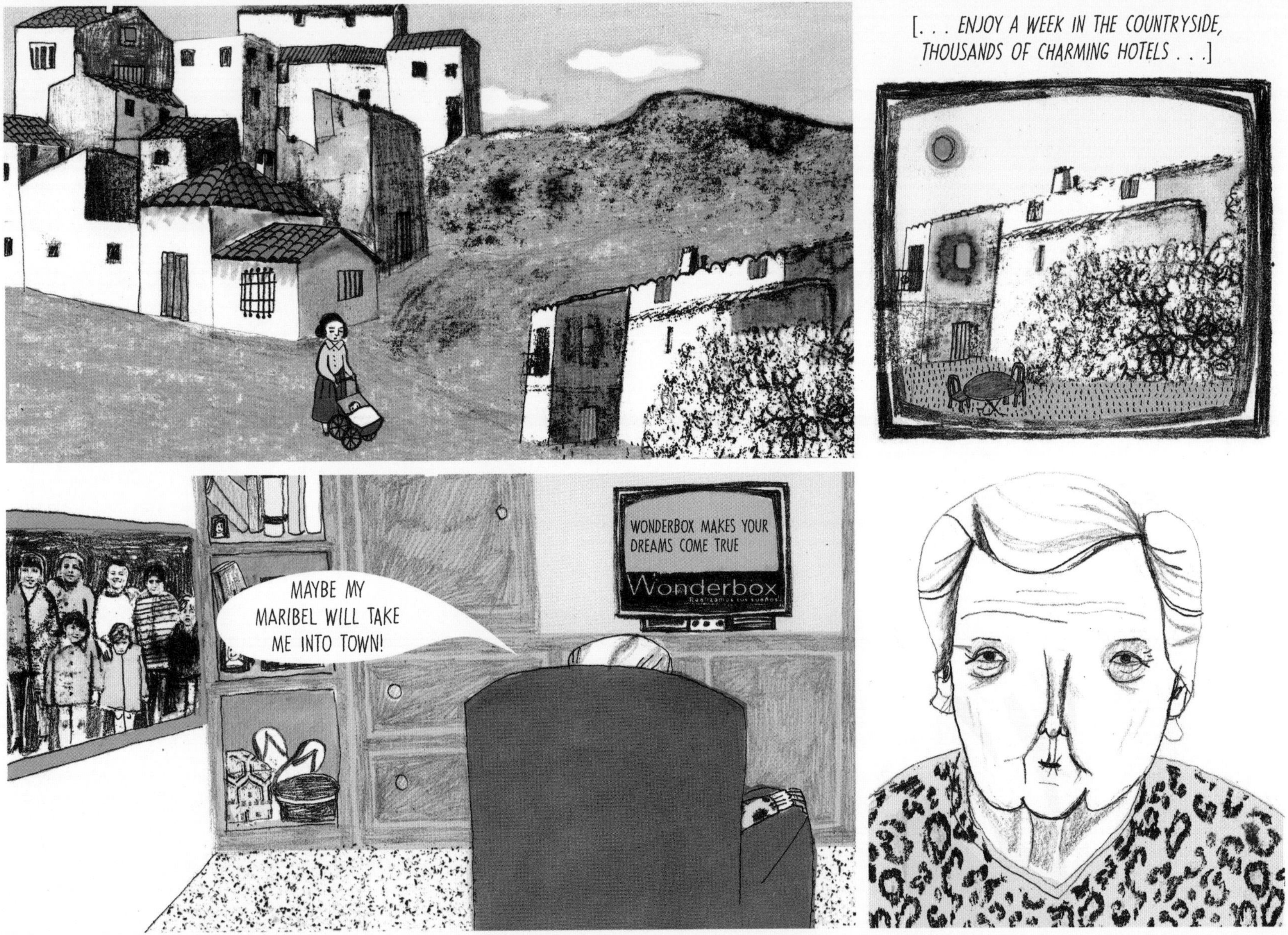
[. . . ENJOY A WEEK IN THE COUNTRYSIDE, THOUSANDS OF CHARMING HOTELS . . .]
MAYBE MY MARIBEL WILL TAKE ME INTO TOWN!
WONDERBOX MAKES YOUR DREAMS COME TRUE
Wonderbox

HERMINIA

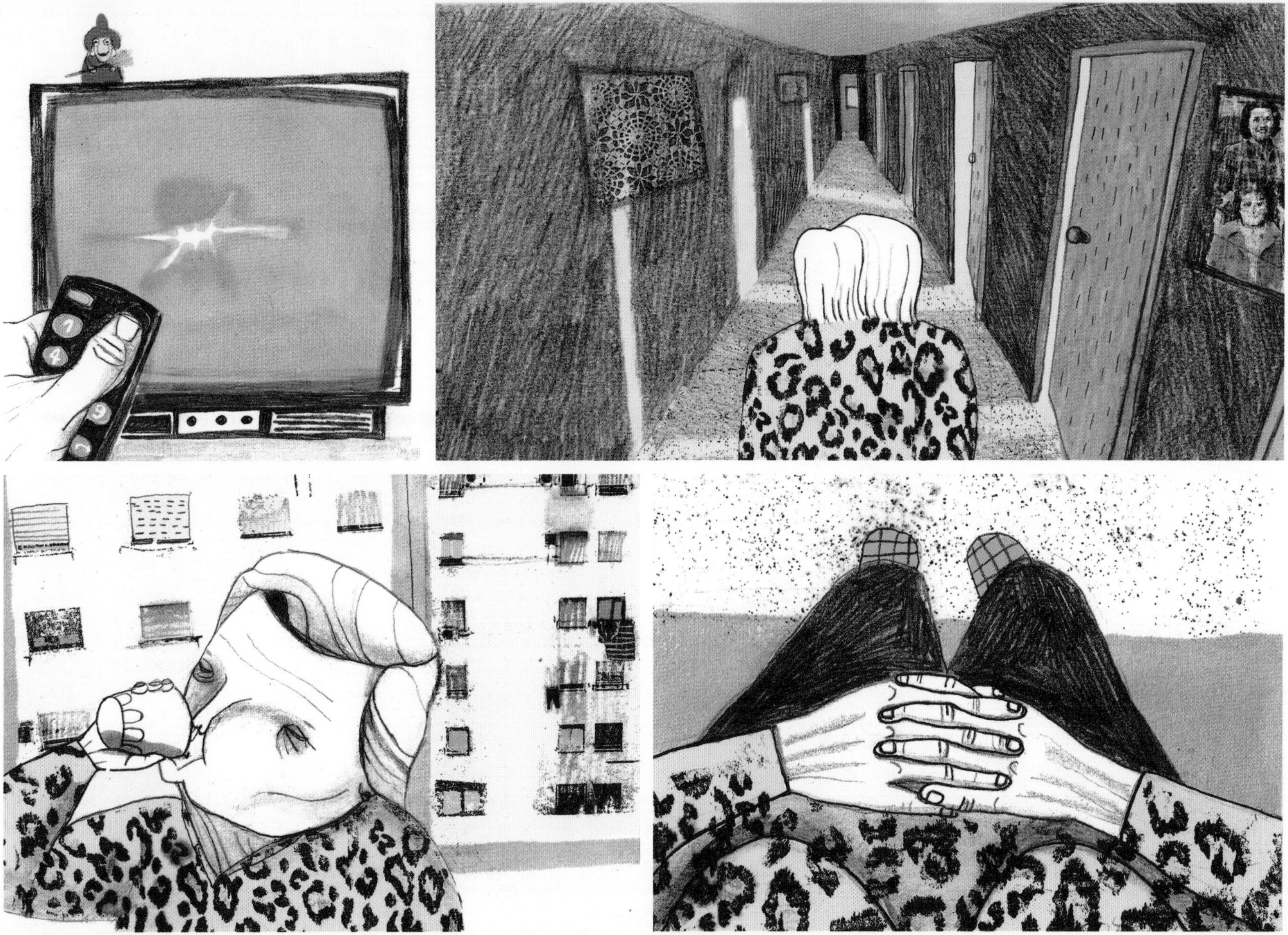

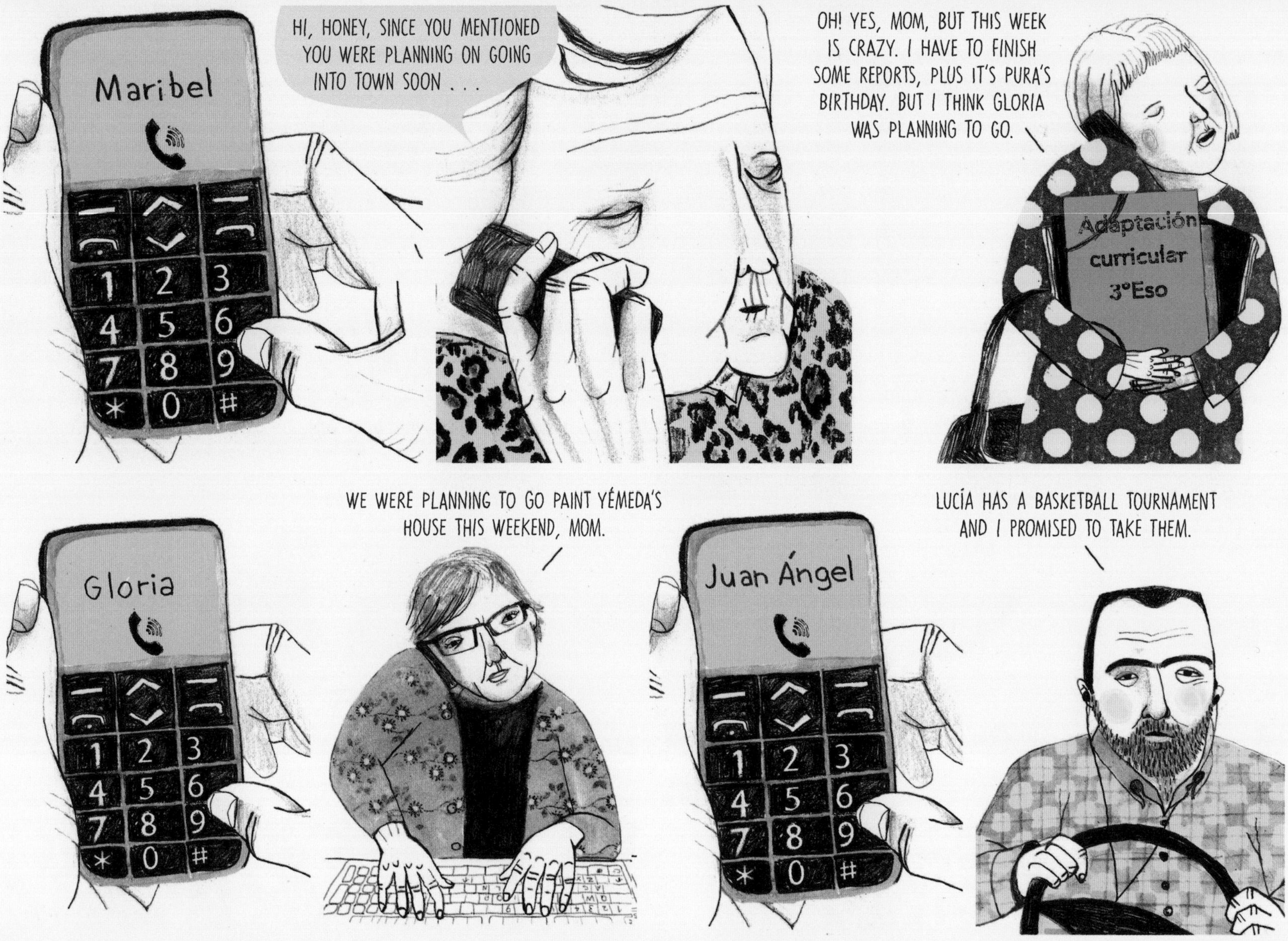

Maribel
HI, HONEY, SINCE YOU MENTIONED YOU WERE PLANNING ON GOING INTO TOWN SOON . . .
OH! YES, MOM, BUT THIS WEEK IS CRAZY. I HAVE TO FINISH SOME REPORTS, PLUS IT'S PURA'S BIRTHDAY. BUT I THINK GLORIA WAS PLANNING TO GO.
Adaptación curricular 3°Eso
Gloria
WE WERE PLANNING TO GO PAINT YÉMEDA'S HOUSE THIS WEEKEND, MOM.
Juan Ángel
LUCÍA HAS A BASKETBALL TOURNAMENT AND I PROMISED TO TAKE THEM.

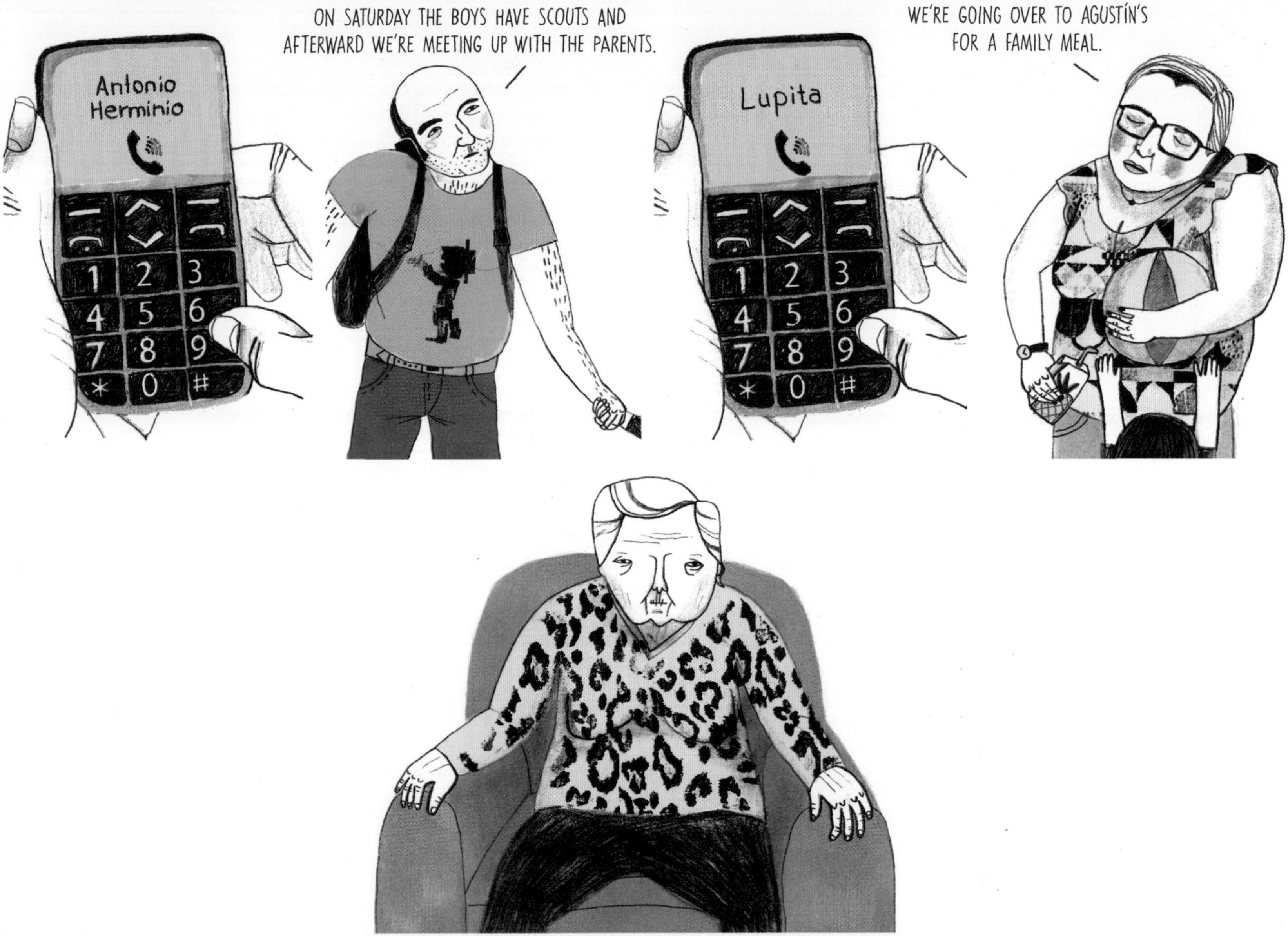
Antonio
Herminio
ON SATURDAY THE BOYS HAVE SCOUTS AND AFTERWARD WE'RE MEETING UP WITH THE PARENTS.
Lupita
WE'RE GOING OVER TO AGUSTÍN'S FOR A FAMILY MEAL.

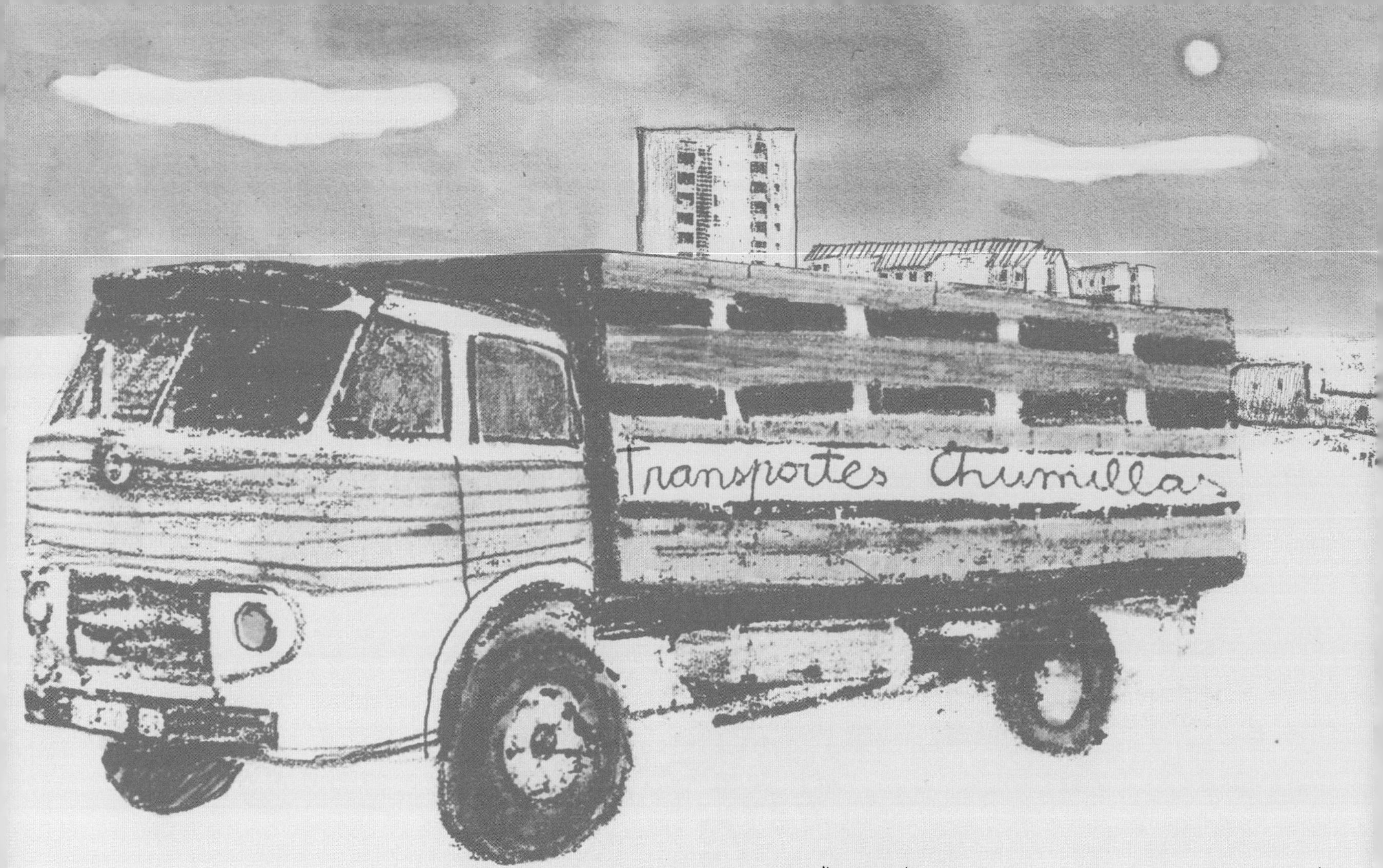
Transportes Chumillas

"I DIDN'T WANT TO, I WAS SORRY TO LEAVE."

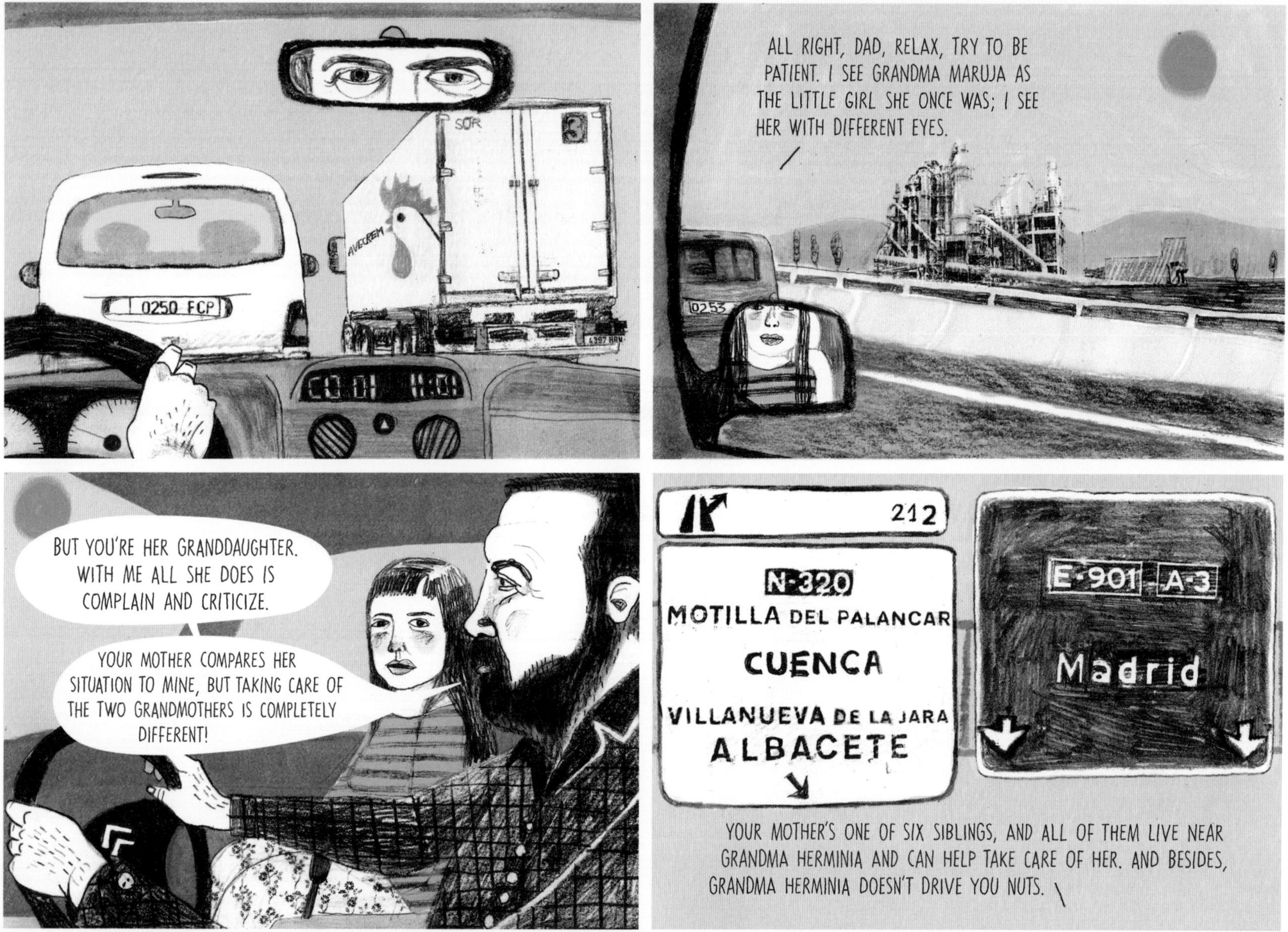

ALL RIGHT, DAD, RELAX, TRY TO BE PATIENT. I SEE GRANDMA MARUJA AS THE LITTLE GIRL SHE ONCE WAS; I SEE HER WITH DIFFERENT EYES.
BUT YOU'RE HER GRANDDAUGHTER. WITH ME ALL SHE DOES IS COMPLAIN AND CRITICIZE.
YOUR MOTHER COMPARES HER SITUATION TO MINE, BUT TAKING CARE OF THE TWO GRANDMOTHERS IS COMPLETELY DIFFERENT!
212
N-320
MOTILLA DEL PALANCAR
CUENCA
VILLANUEVA DE LA JARA
ALBACETE
E-901 A-3
Madrid
YOUR MOTHER'S ONE OF SIX SIBLINGS, AND ALL OF THEM LIVE NEAR GRANDMA HERMINIA AND CAN HELP TAKE CARE OF HER. AND BESIDES, GRANDMA HERMINIA DOESN'T DRIVE YOU NUTS.

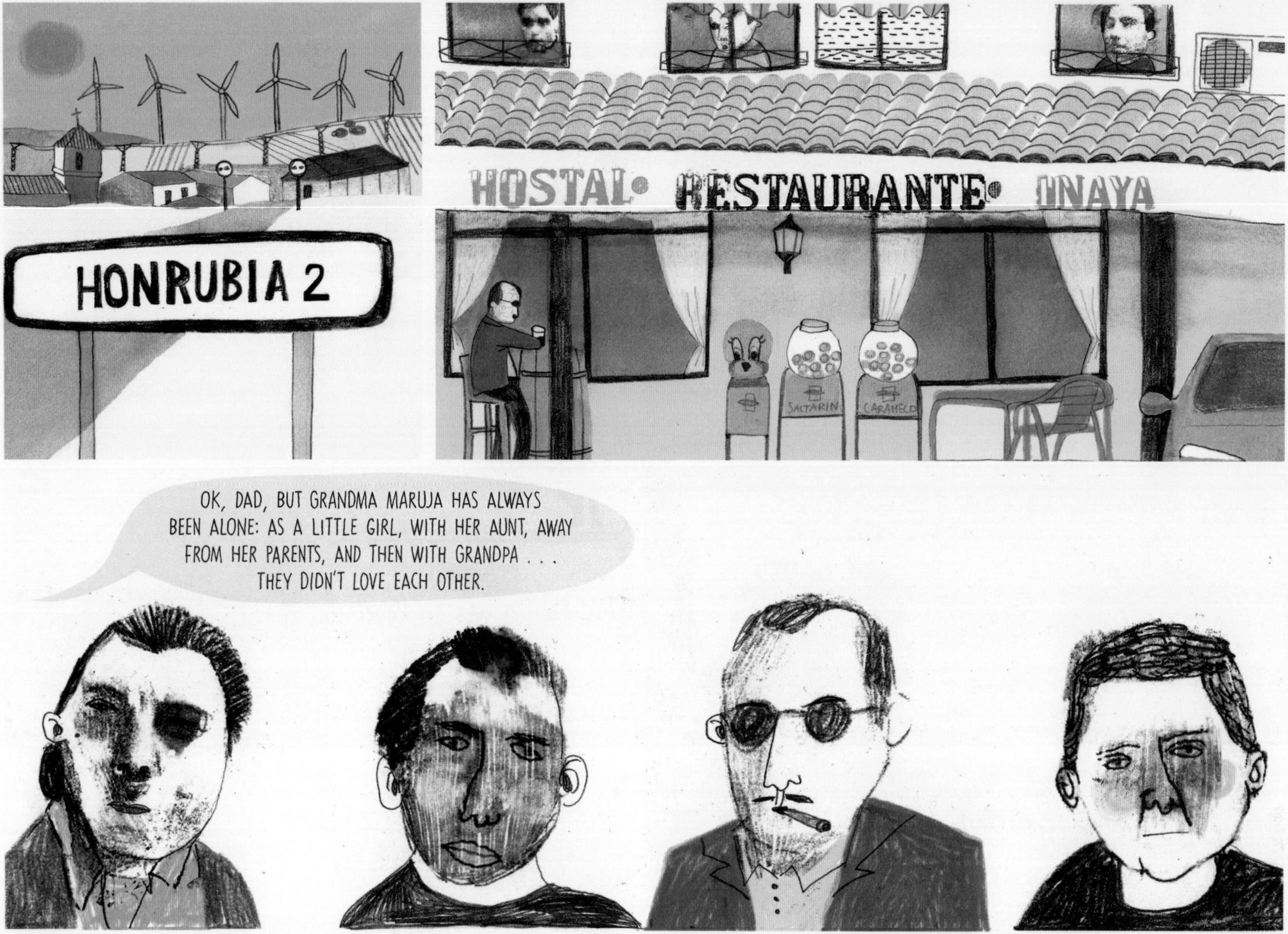
HOSTAL RESTAURANTE ONAYA
SALTARIN
CARAMELO
HONRUBIA 2
OK, DAD, BUT GRANDMA MARUJA HAS ALWAYS BEEN ALONE: AS A LITTLE GIRL, WITH HER AUNT, AWAY FROM HER PARENTS, AND THEN WITH GRANDPA . . . THEY DIDN'T LOVE EACH OTHER.

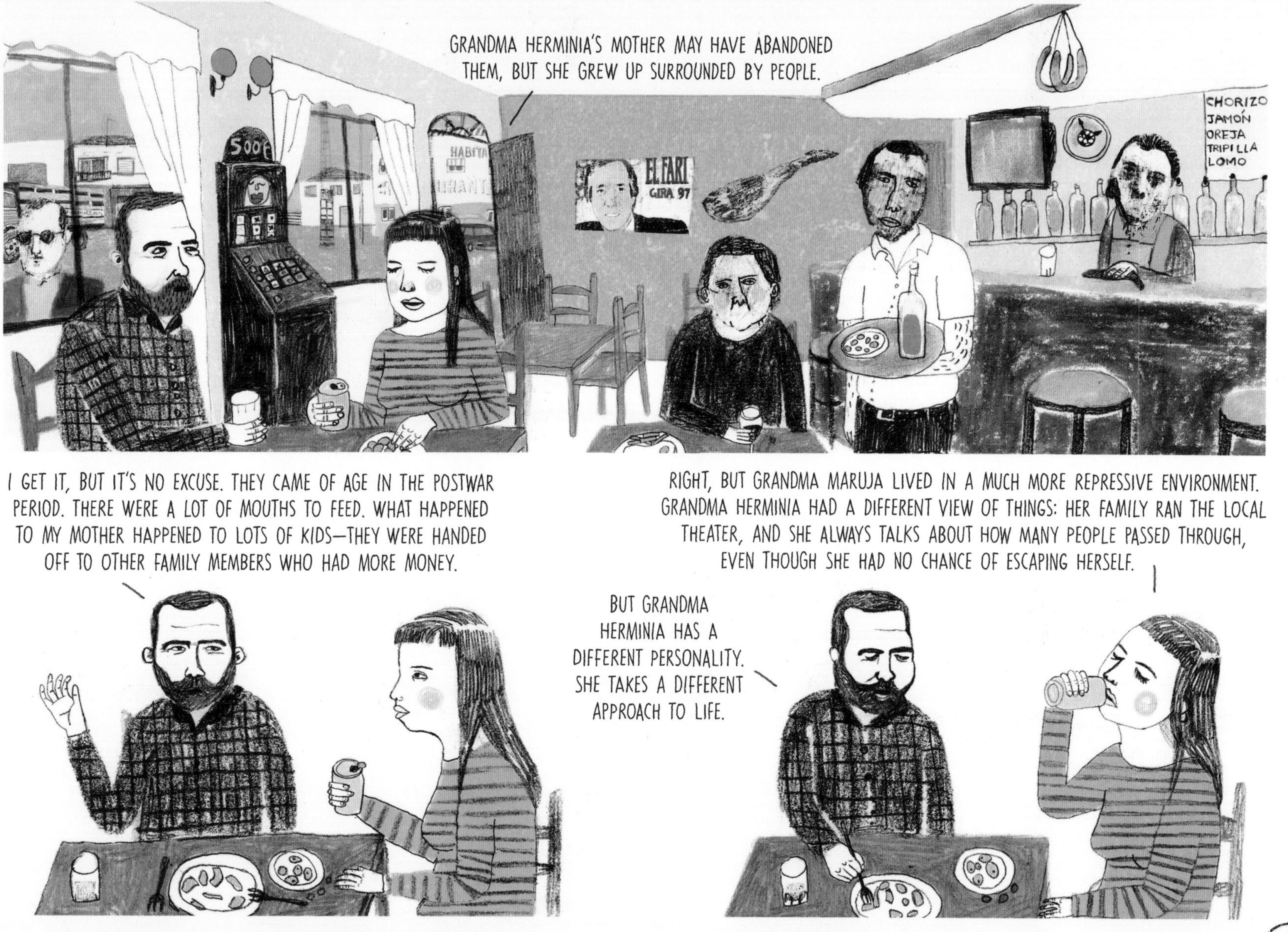

GRANDMA HERMINIA'S MOTHER MAY HAVE ABANDONED THEM, BUT SHE GREW UP SURROUNDED BY PEOPLE.
500€
EL FARI
GIRA 97
CHORIZO
JAMÓN
OREJA
TRIPILLA
LOMO
I GET IT, BUT IT'S NO EXCUSE. THEY CAME OF AGE IN THE POSTWAR PERIOD. THERE WERE A LOT OF MOUTHS TO FEED. WHAT HAPPENED TO MY MOTHER HAPPENED TO LOTS OF KIDS—THEY WERE HANDED OFF TO OTHER FAMILY MEMBERS WHO HAD MORE MONEY.
RIGHT, BUT GRANDMA MARUJA LIVED IN A MUCH MORE REPRESSIVE ENVIRONMENT. GRANDMA HERMINIA HAD A DIFFERENT VIEW OF THINGS: HER FAMILY RAN THE LOCAL THEATER, AND SHE ALWAYS TALKS ABOUT HOW MANY PEOPLE PASSED THROUGH, EVEN THOUGH SHE HAD NO CHANCE OF ESCAPING HERSELF.
BUT GRANDMA HERMINIA HAS A DIFFERENT PERSONALITY. SHE TAKES A DIFFERENT APPROACH TO LIFE.

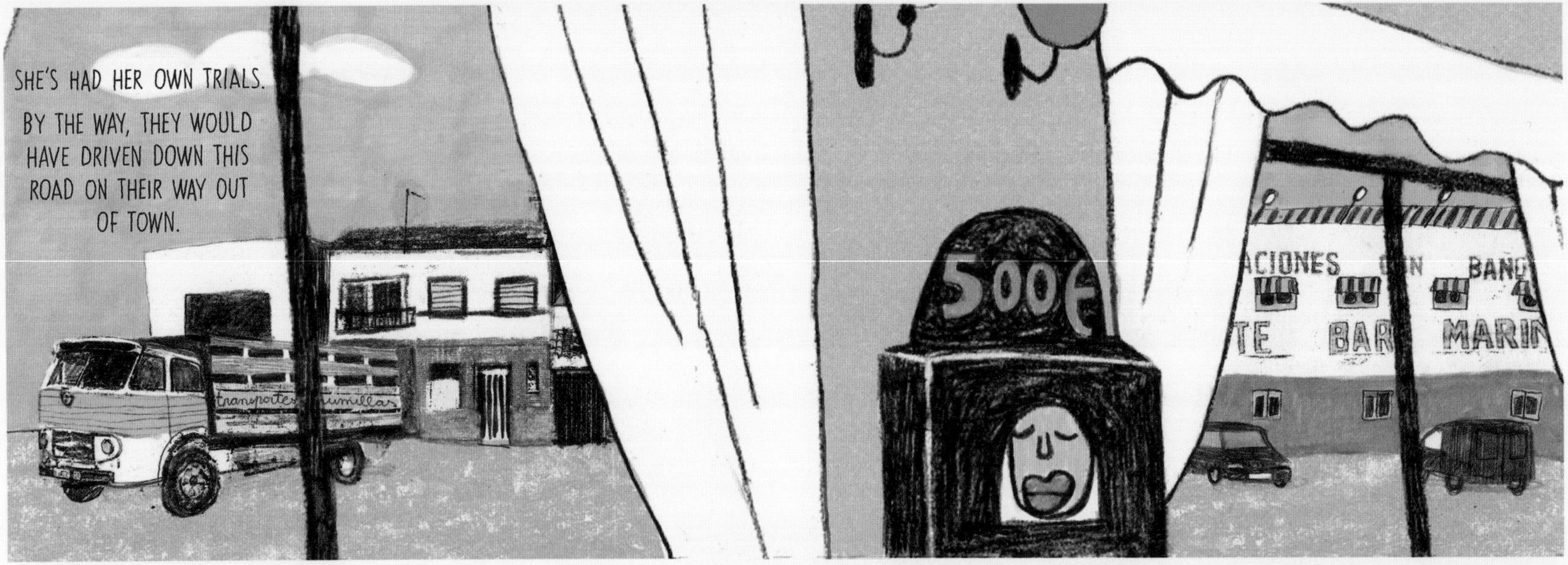
SHE'S HAD HER OWN TRIALS.
BY THE WAY, THEY WOULD HAVE DRIVEN DOWN THIS ROAD ON THEIR WAY OUT OF TOWN.
transportes chumillas
500€
BAR

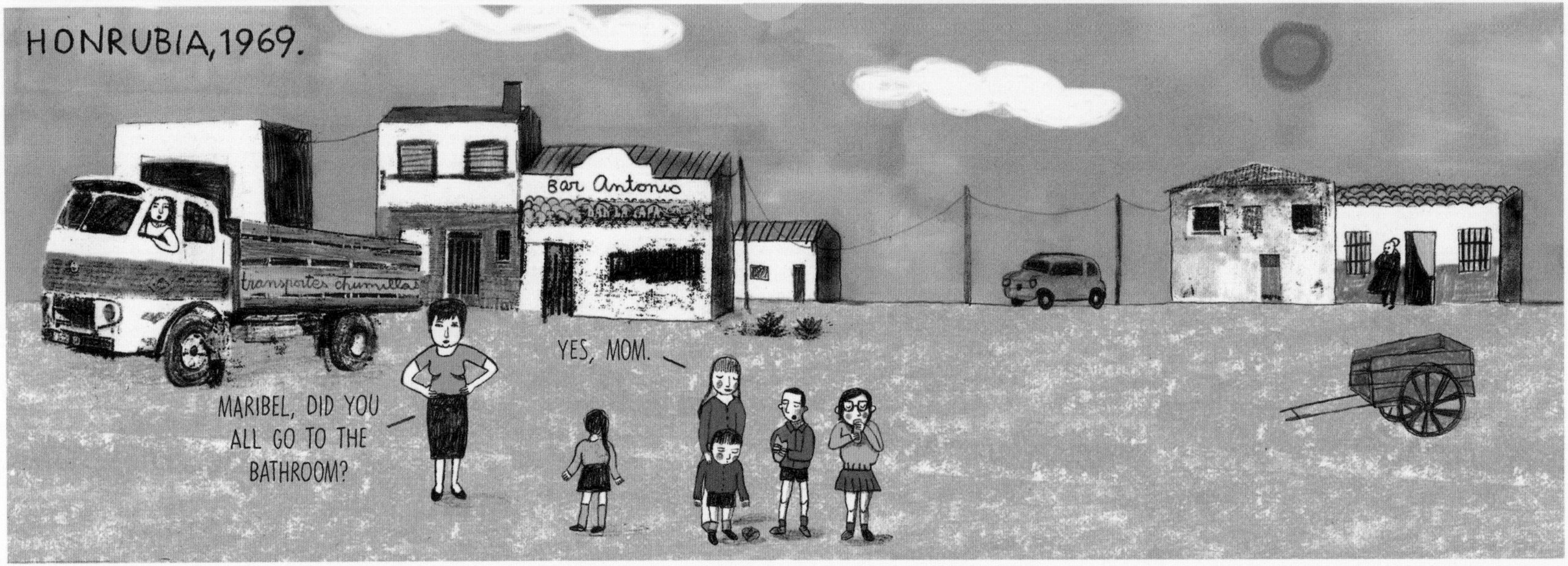
HONRUBIA, 1969.
Bar Antonio
transportes chumillas
MARIBEL, DID YOU ALL GO TO THE BATHROOM?
YES, MOM.

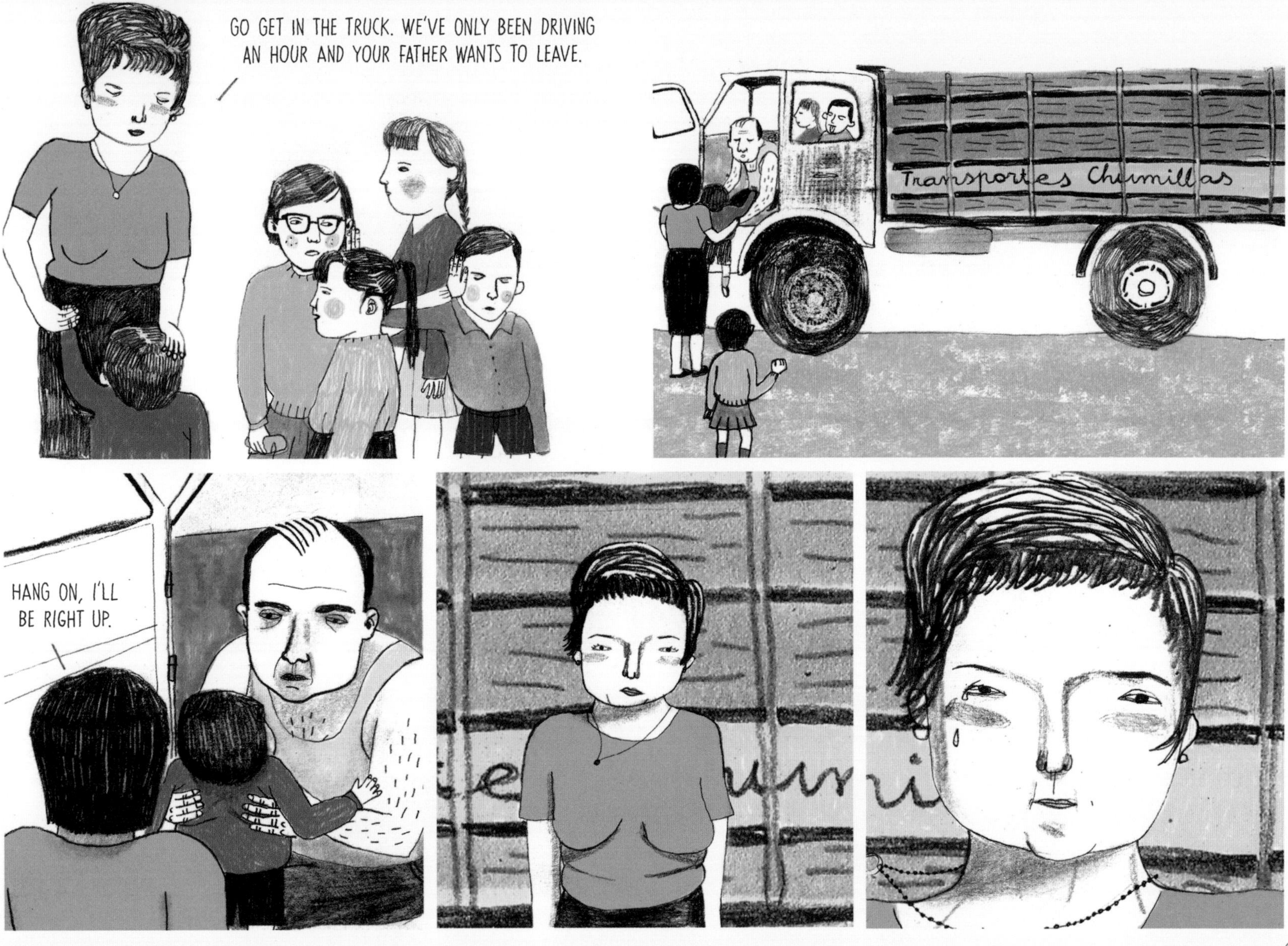
GO GET IN THE TRUCK. WE'VE ONLY BEEN DRIVING AN HOUR AND YOUR FATHER WANTS TO LEAVE.
Transportes Chumillas
HANG ON, I'LL BE RIGHT UP.

♫ A RAY OF SUNSHINE, OH, OH, OH! ♫

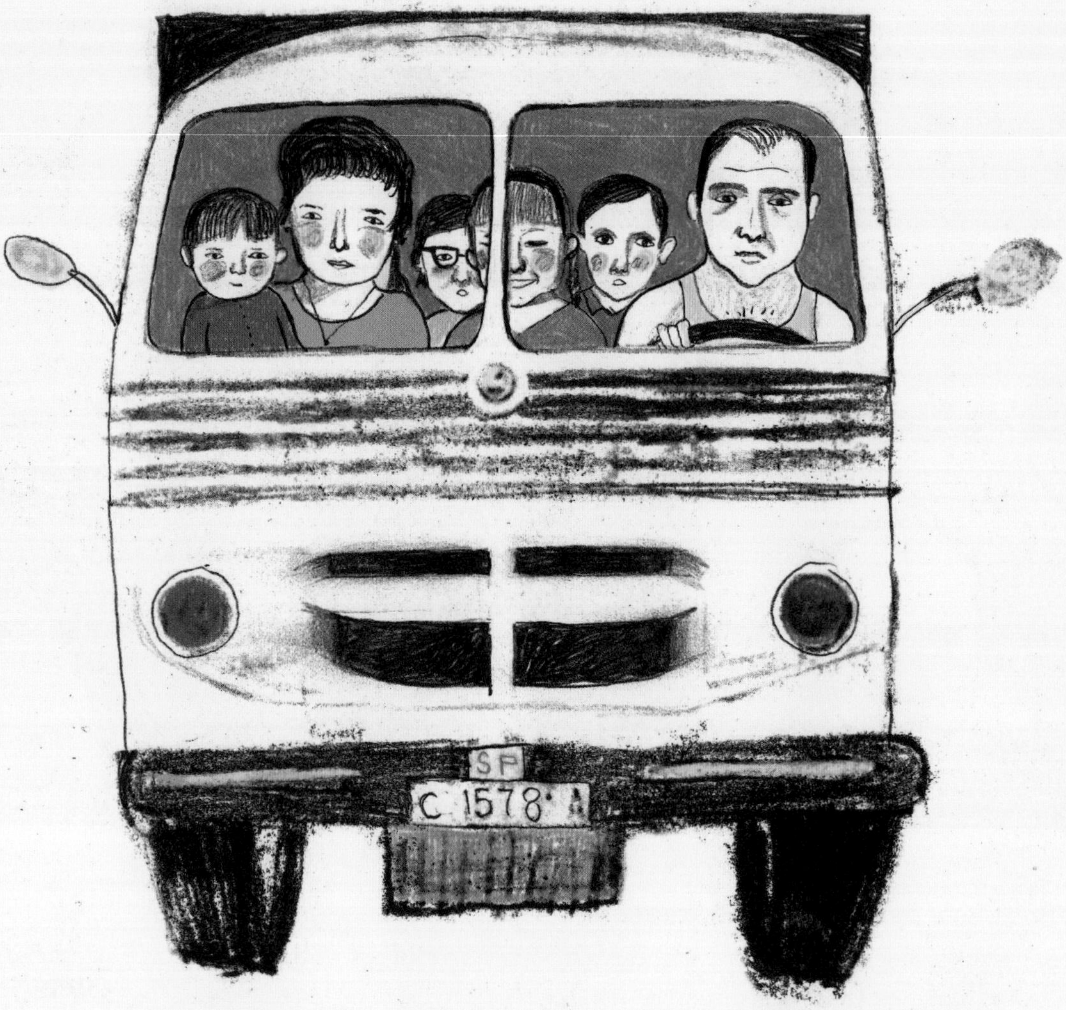

SP
C 1578 A

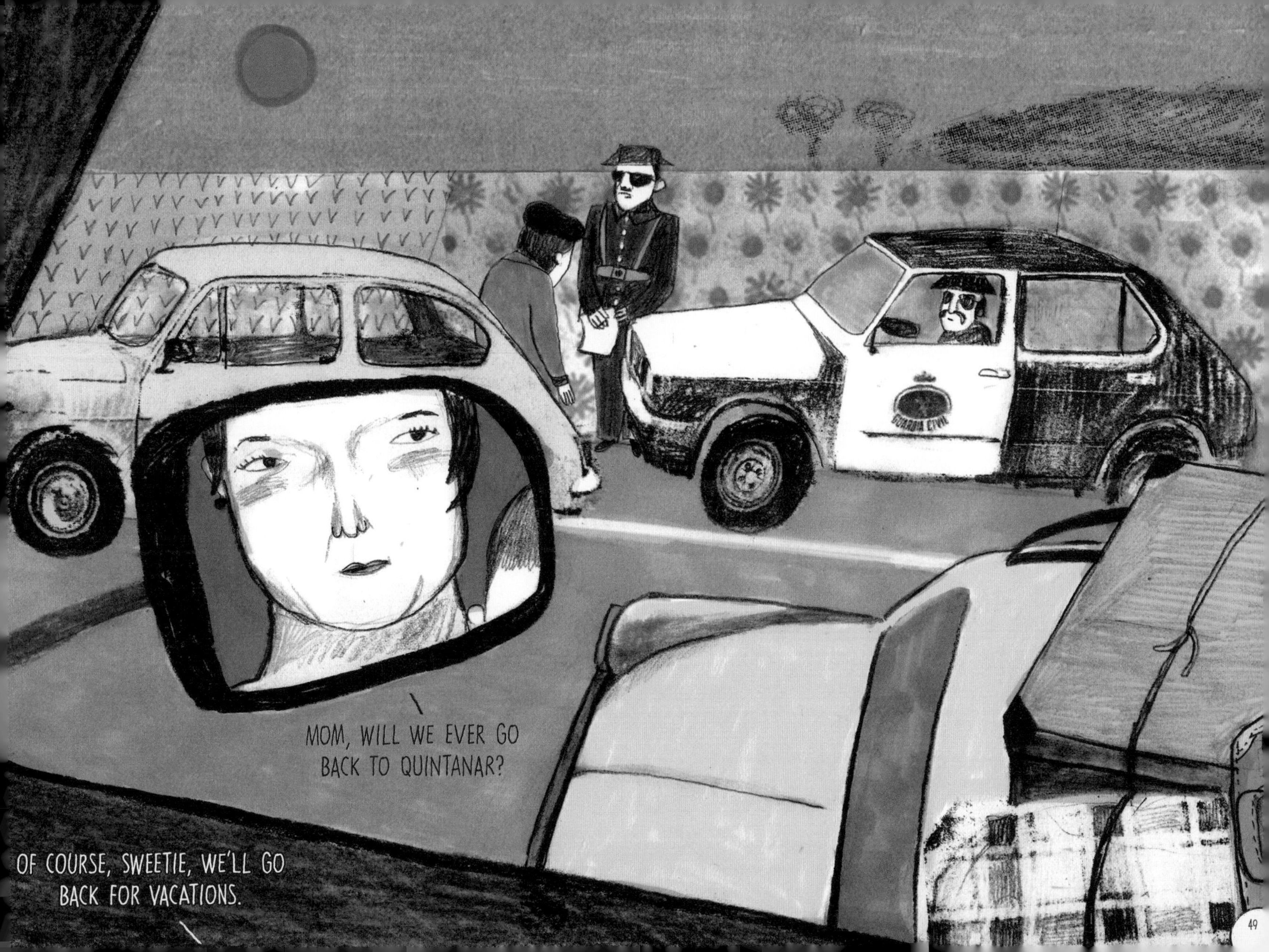
MOM, WILL WE EVER GO BACK TO QUINTANAR?
OF COURSE, SWEETIE, WE'LL GO BACK FOR VACATIONS.
GUARDIA CIVIL

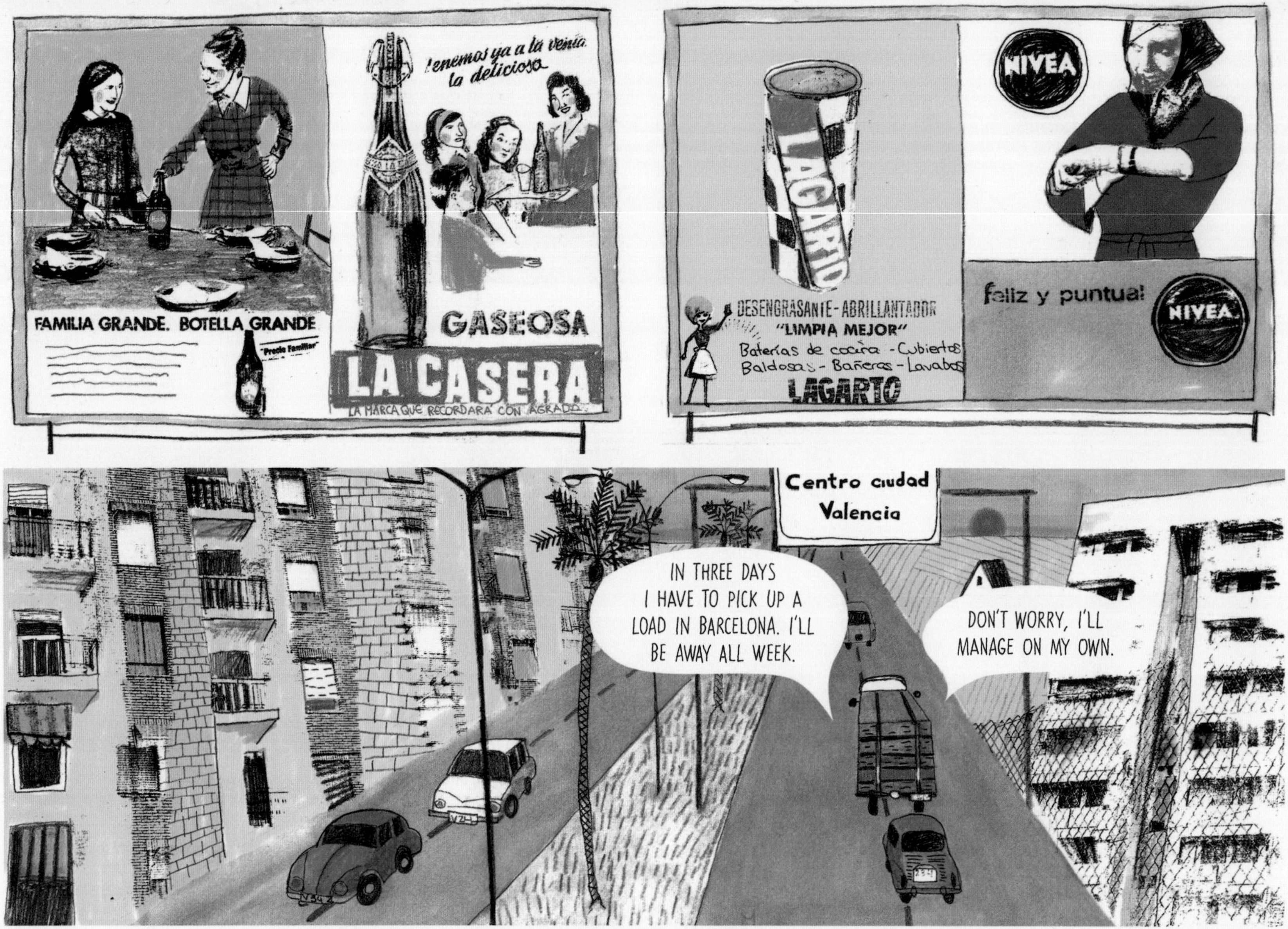
Tenemos ya a la venta la deliciosa
FAMILIA GRANDE. BOTELLA GRANDE
"Precio Familiar"
GASEOSA
LA CASERA
LA MARCA QUE RECORDARA CON AGRADO
NIVEA
DESENGRASANTE-ABRILLANTADOR
"LIMPIA MEJOR"
Baterías de cocina - Cubiertos
Baldosas - Bañeras - Lavabos
LAGARTO
feliz y puntual
NIVEA
Centro ciudad
Valencia
IN THREE DAYS I HAVE TO PICK UP A LOAD IN BARCELONA. I'LL BE AWAY ALL WEEK.
DON'T WORRY, I'LL MANAGE ON MY OWN.

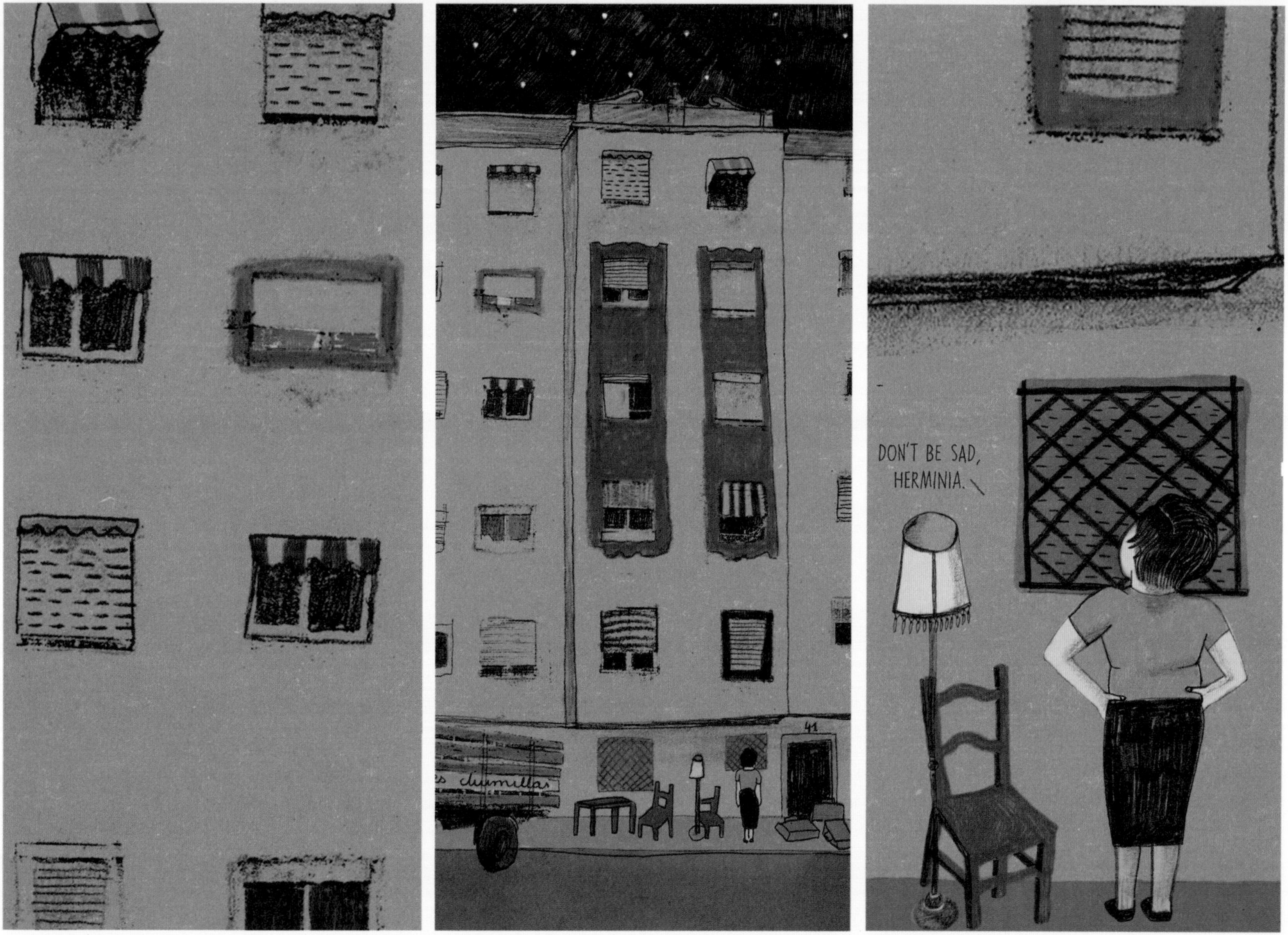
41
DON'T BE SAD, HERMINIA.

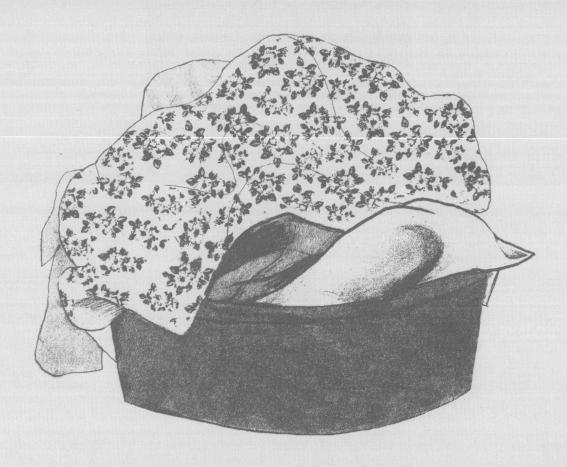

"I FIRST HAD A WASHING MACHINE WHEN THEY INSTALLED ONE AT THE FARM.
I WAS USED TO WASHING BY HAND . . . WHAT DO I KNOW . . . IT'S TRUE,
I'VE DONE PLENTY OF WASHING . . . I'VE BEEN STRONG."

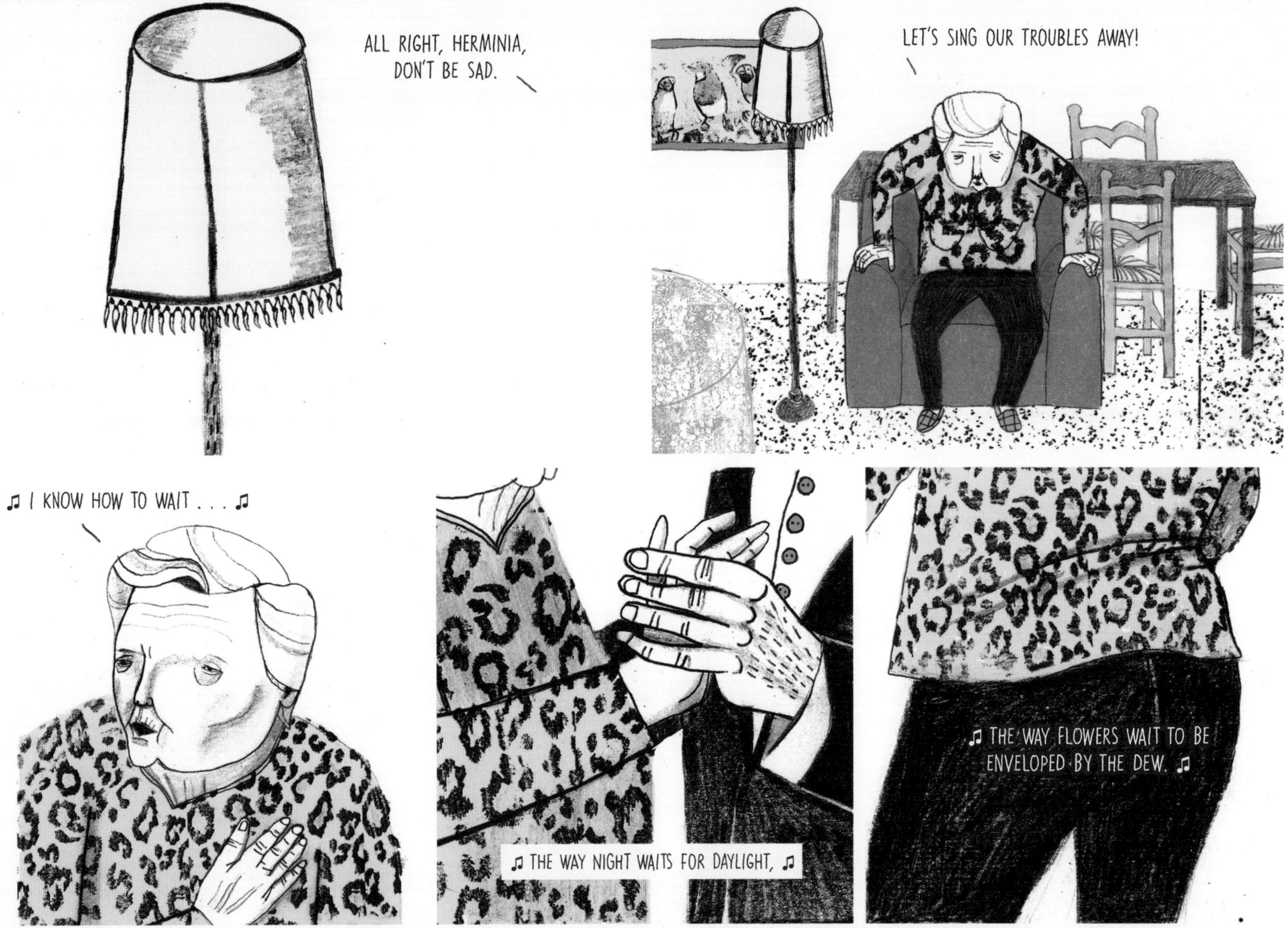
ALL RIGHT, HERMINIA, DON'T BE SAD.
LET'S SING OUR TROUBLES AWAY!
♫ I KNOW HOW TO WAIT . . . ♫
♫ THE WAY NIGHT WAITS FOR DAYLIGHT, ♫
♫ THE WAY FLOWERS WAIT TO BE ENVELOPED BY THE DEW. ♫

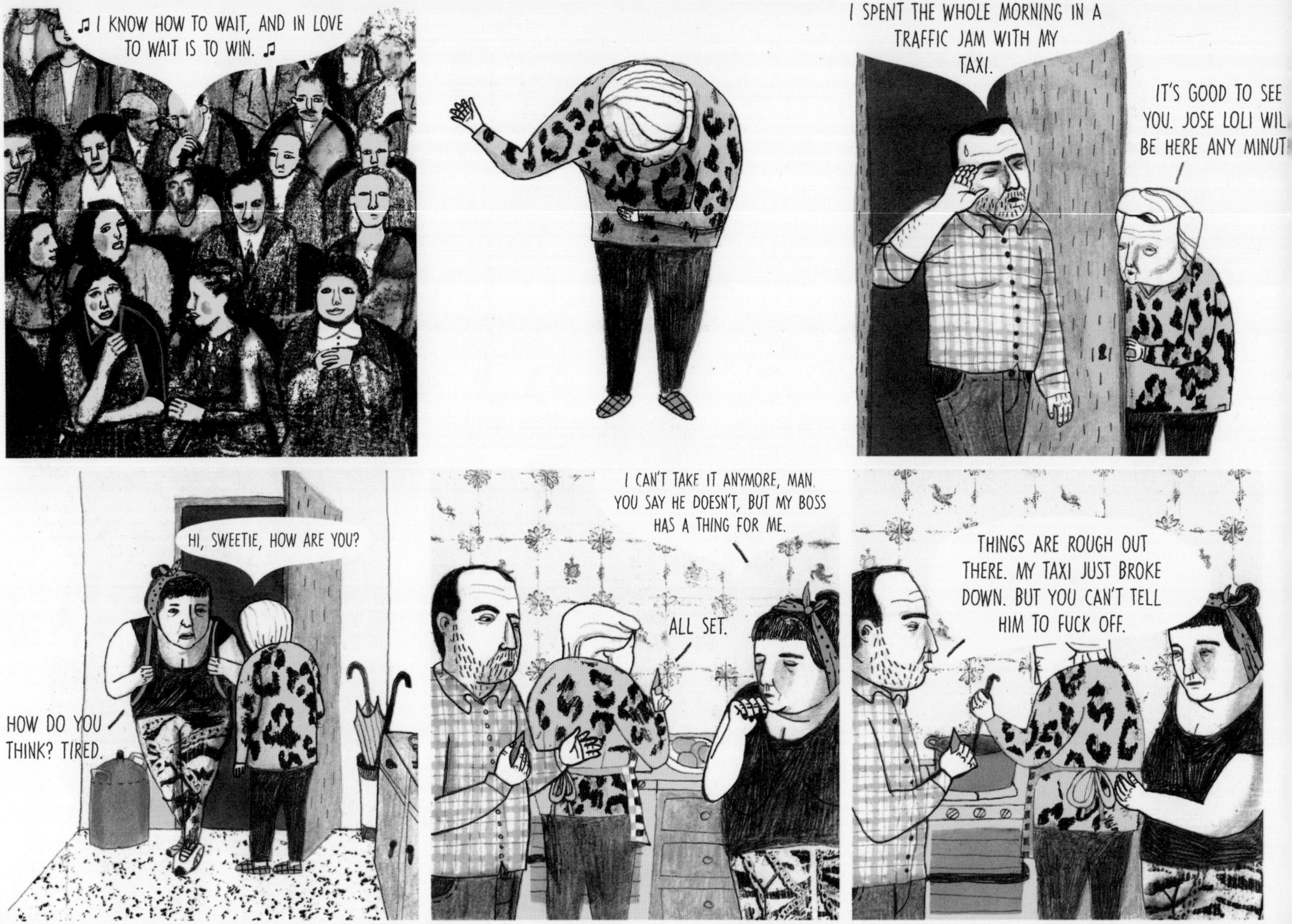
♫ I KNOW HOW TO WAIT, AND IN LOVE TO WAIT IS TO WIN. ♫
I SPENT THE WHOLE MORNING IN A TRAFFIC JAM WITH MY TAXI.
IT'S GOOD TO SEE YOU. JOSE LOLI WIL BE HERE ANY MINUT
HI, SWEETIE, HOW ARE YOU?
HOW DO YOU THINK? TIRED.
I CAN'T TAKE IT ANYMORE, MAN. YOU SAY HE DOESN'T, BUT MY BOSS HAS A THING FOR ME.
ALL SET.
THINGS ARE ROUGH OUT THERE. MY TAXI JUST BROKE DOWN. BUT YOU CAN'T TELL HIM TO FUCK OFF.

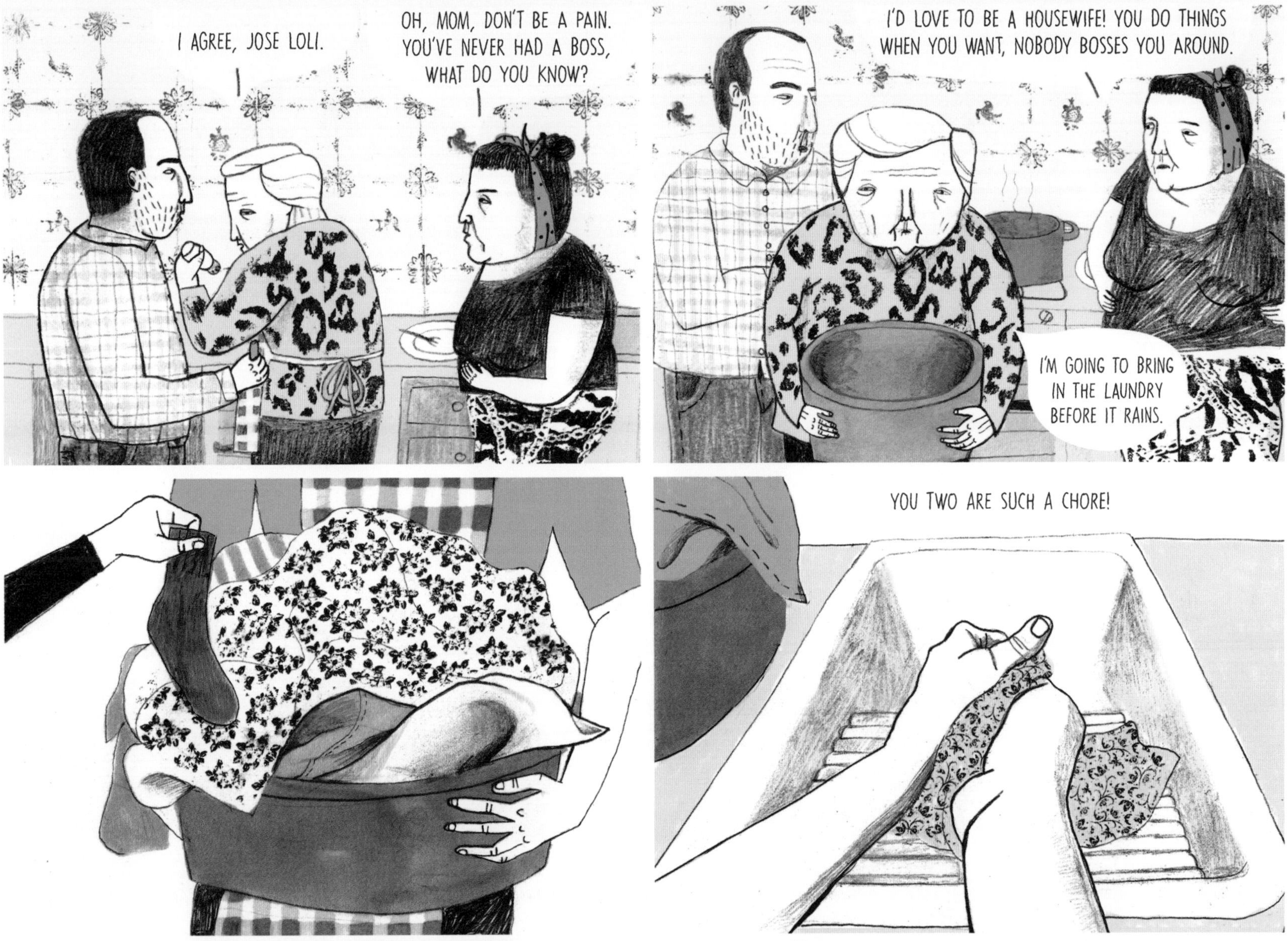
I AGREE, JOSE LOLI.
OH, MOM, DON'T BE A PAIN. YOU'VE NEVER HAD A BOSS, WHAT DO YOU KNOW?
I'D LOVE TO BE A HOUSEWIFE! YOU DO THINGS WHEN YOU WANT, NOBODY BOSSES YOU AROUND.
I'M GOING TO BRING IN THE LAUNDRY BEFORE IT RAINS.
YOU TWO ARE SUCH A CHORE!

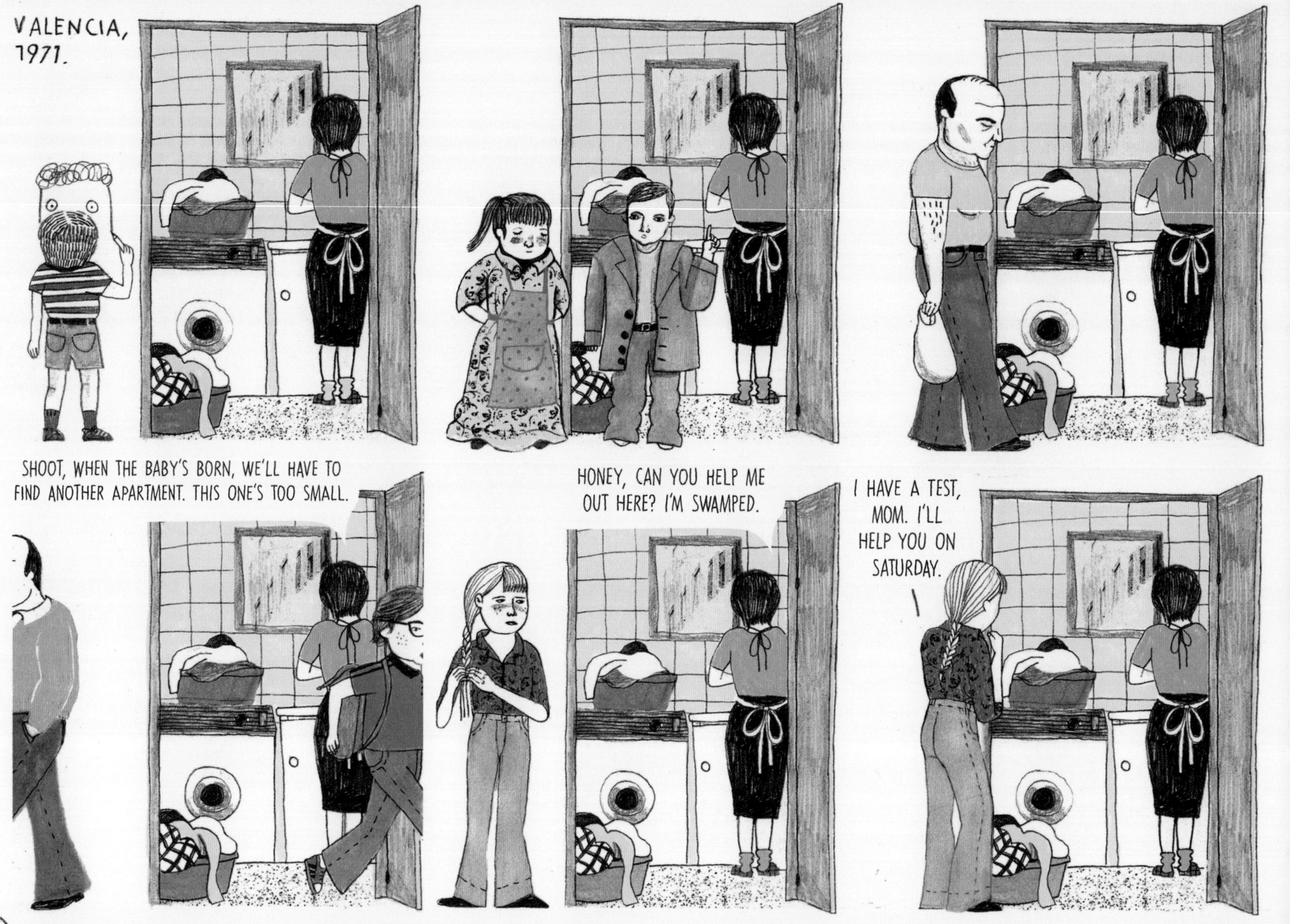
VALENCIA, 1971.
SHOOT, WHEN THE BABY'S BORN, WE'LL HAVE TO FIND ANOTHER APARTMENT. THIS ONE'S TOO SMALL.
HONEY, CAN YOU HELP ME OUT HERE? I'M SWAMPED.
I HAVE A TEST, MOM. I'LL HELP YOU ON SATURDAY.

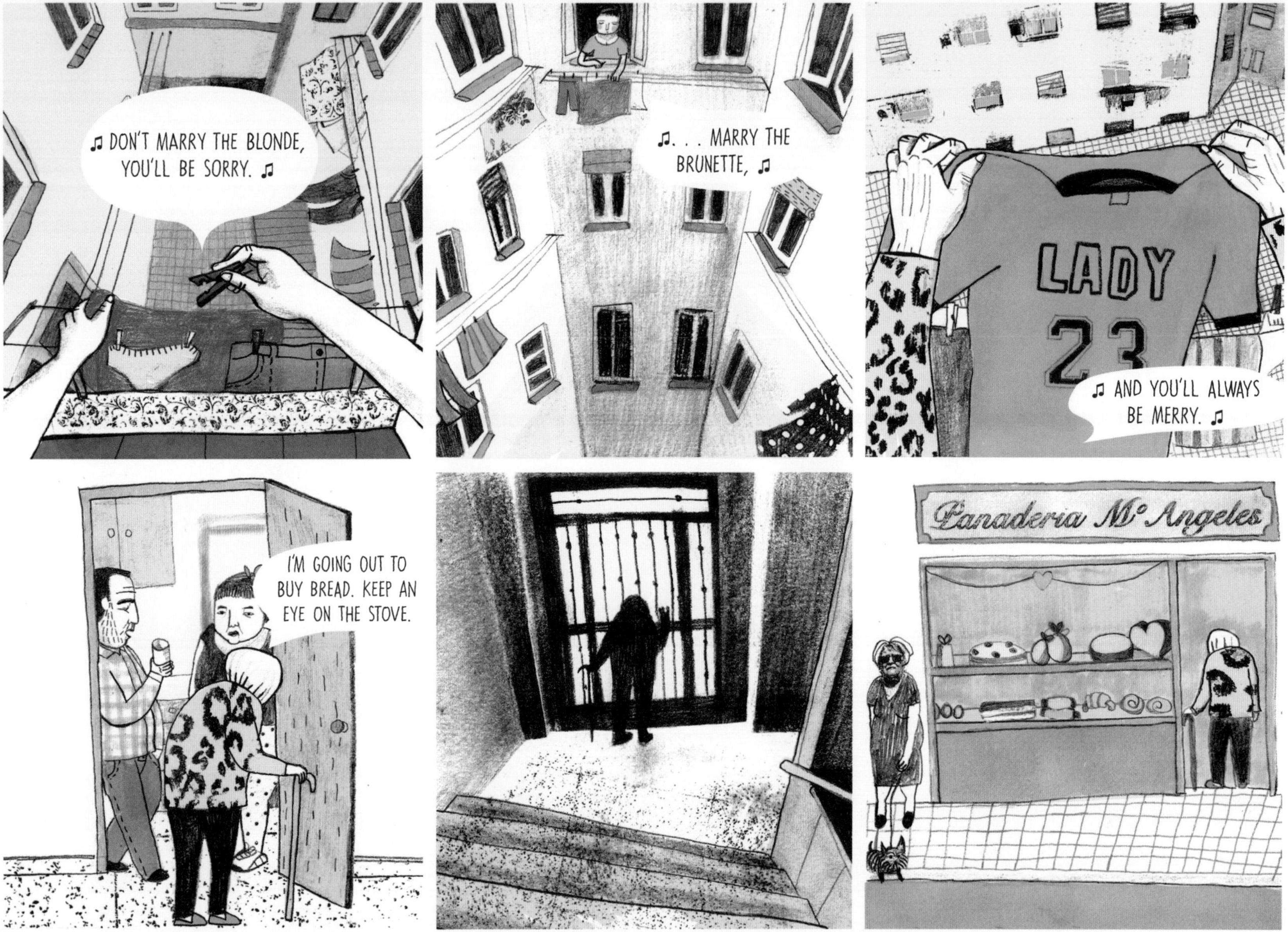
♫ DON'T MARRY THE BLONDE, YOU'LL BE SORRY. ♫
♫. . . MARRY THE BRUNETTE, ♫
LADY
23
♫ AND YOU'LL ALWAYS BE MERRY. ♫
I'M GOING OUT TO BUY BREAD. KEEP AN EYE ON THE STOVE.
Panaderia Mª Angeles

LA VOZ OBRERA

OPOSICIÓN DE IZQUIERDA DEL PARTIDO COMUNISTA DE ESPAÑA (OPI)
DIRECCIÓN NACIONAL DEL PAÍS VALENCIANO

| Nº 6 (IIª EPOCA) | ABRIL 1974 | 10 Ptas. |

CONSTITUCIÓN DE LAS JUVENTUDES

"YOUR MOTHER AND AUNT USED TO GO AROUND POSTING PROPAGANDA, AND WE'D BEEN THROUGH A WAR. WE WERE SCARED NO MATTER WHAT."

Maribel Chamillas

58

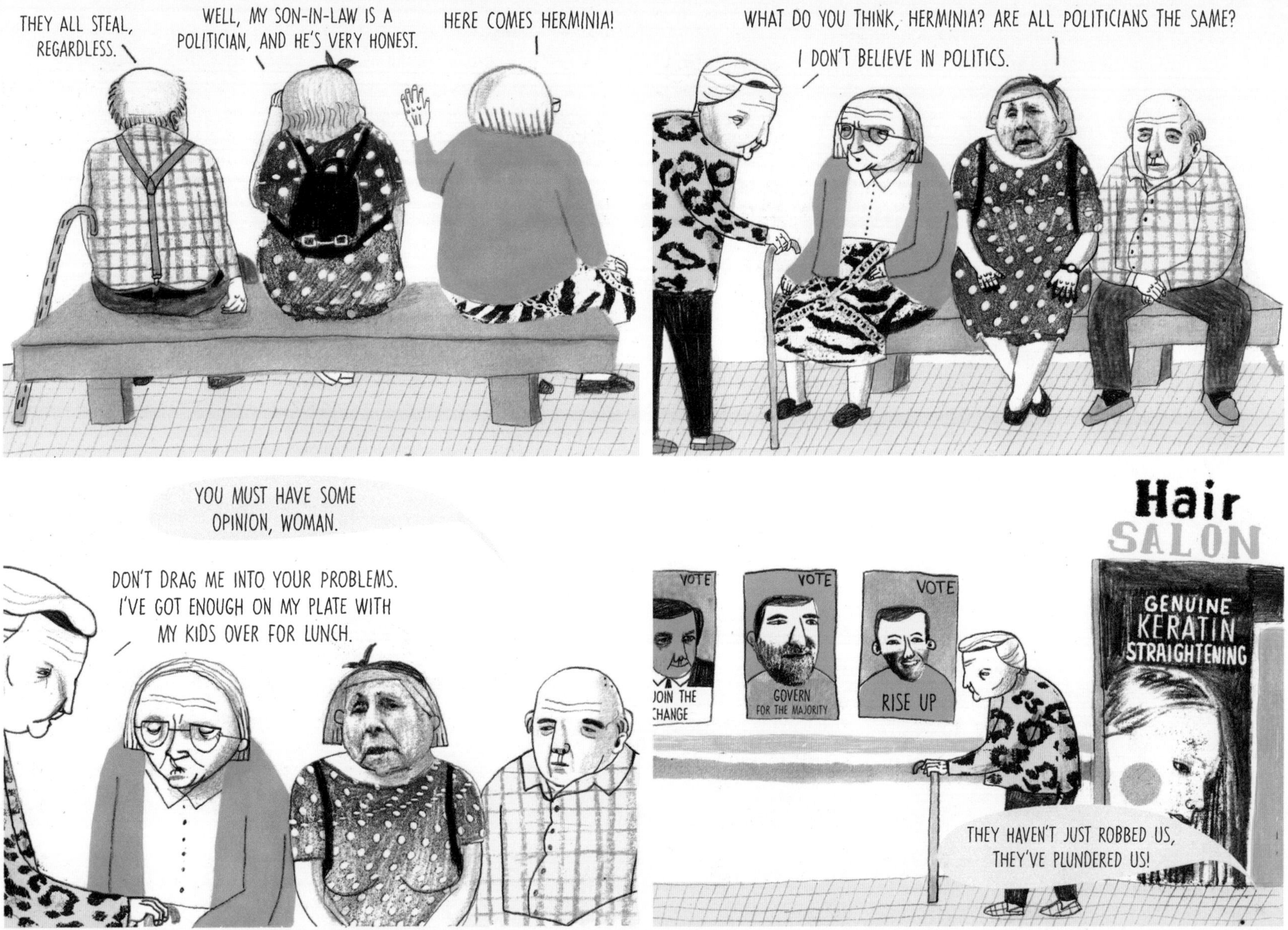
THEY ALL STEAL, REGARDLESS.
WELL, MY SON-IN-LAW IS A POLITICIAN, AND HE'S VERY HONEST.
HERE COMES HERMINIA!
WHAT DO YOU THINK, HERMINIA? ARE ALL POLITICIANS THE SAME?
I DON'T BELIEVE IN POLITICS.
YOU MUST HAVE SOME OPINION, WOMAN.
DON'T DRAG ME INTO YOUR PROBLEMS. I'VE GOT ENOUGH ON MY PLATE WITH MY KIDS OVER FOR LUNCH.
VOTE
VOTE
GOVERN FOR THE MAJORITY
VOTE
RISE UP
Hair SALON
GENUINE KERATIN STRAIGHTENING
THEY HAVEN'T JUST ROBBED US, THEY'VE PLUNDERED US!

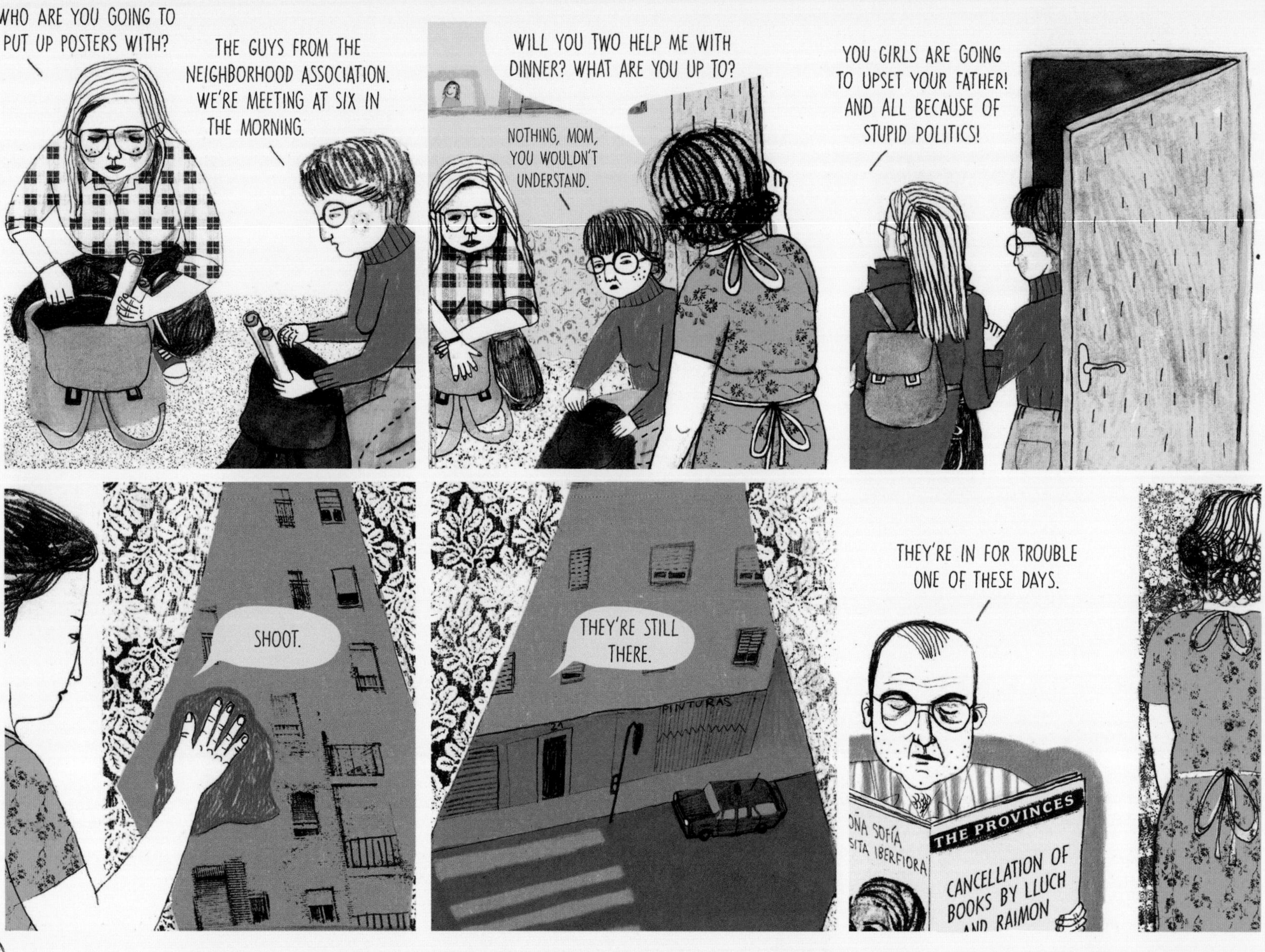
WHO ARE YOU GOING TO PUT UP POSTERS WITH?
THE GUYS FROM THE NEIGHBORHOOD ASSOCIATION. WE'RE MEETING AT SIX IN THE MORNING.
WILL YOU TWO HELP ME WITH DINNER? WHAT ARE YOU UP TO?
NOTHING, MOM, YOU WOULDN'T UNDERSTAND.
YOU GIRLS ARE GOING TO UPSET YOUR FATHER! AND ALL BECAUSE OF STUPID POLITICS!
SHOOT.
THEY'RE STILL THERE.
PINTURAS
THEY'RE IN FOR TROUBLE ONE OF THESE DAYS.
THE PROVINCES
CANCELLATION OF BOOKS BY LLUCH AND RAIMON

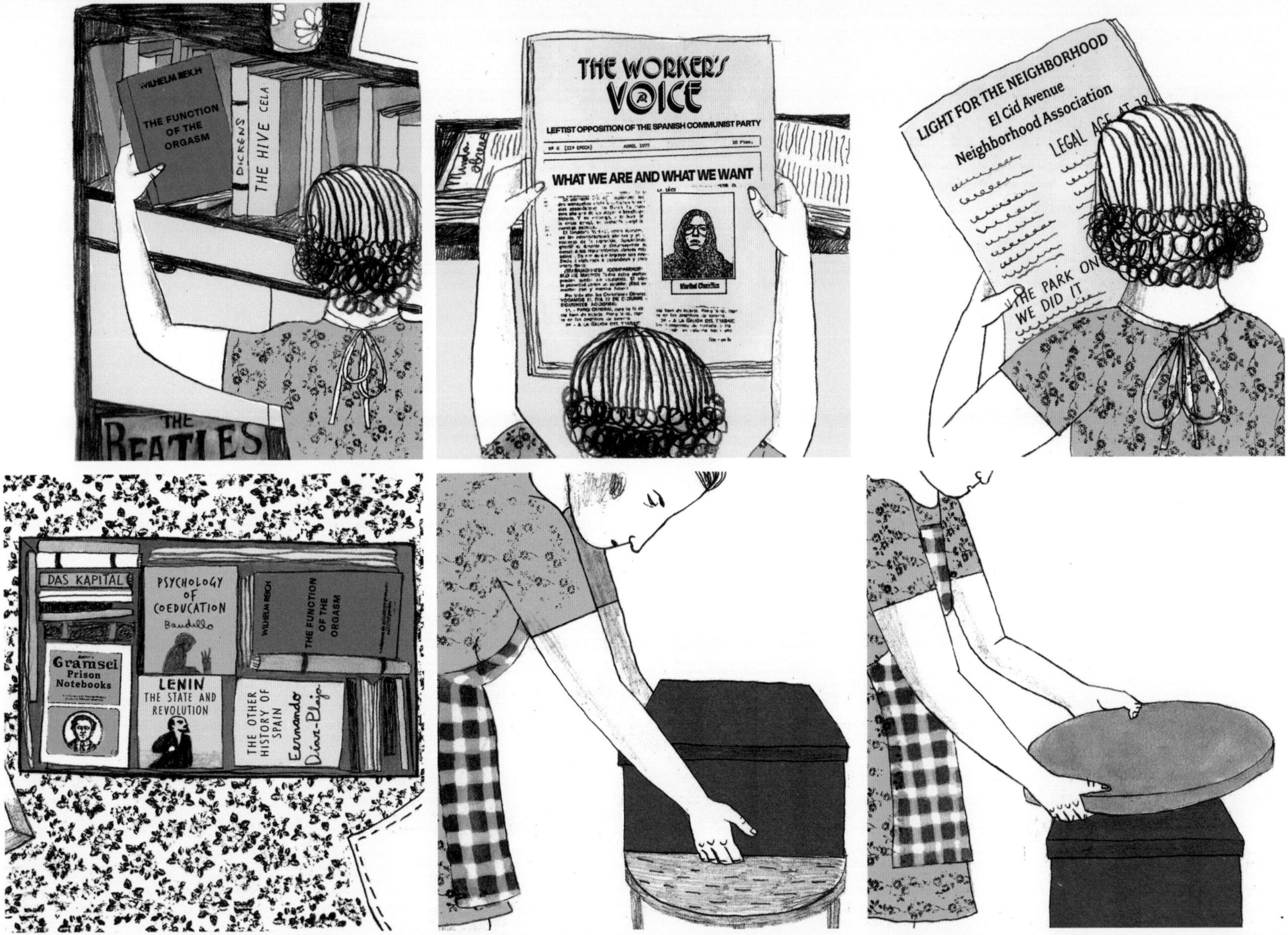

WILHELM REICH
THE FUNCTION OF THE ORGASM
DICKENS
THE HIVE
CELA
THE BEATLES
THE WORKER'S VOICE
LEFTIST OPPOSITION OF THE SPANISH COMMUNIST PARTY
WHAT WE ARE AND WHAT WE WANT
LIGHT FOR THE NEIGHBORHOOD
El Cid Avenue
Neighborhood Association
LEGAL AGE AT 18
THE PARK ON
WE DID IT
DAS KAPITAL
PSYCHOLOGY OF COEDUCATION
Baudillo
WILHELM REICH
THE FUNCTION OF THE ORGASM
Gramsci
Prison Notebooks
LENIN
THE STATE AND REVOLUTION
THE OTHER HISTORY OF SPAIN
Fernando Díaz-Plaja

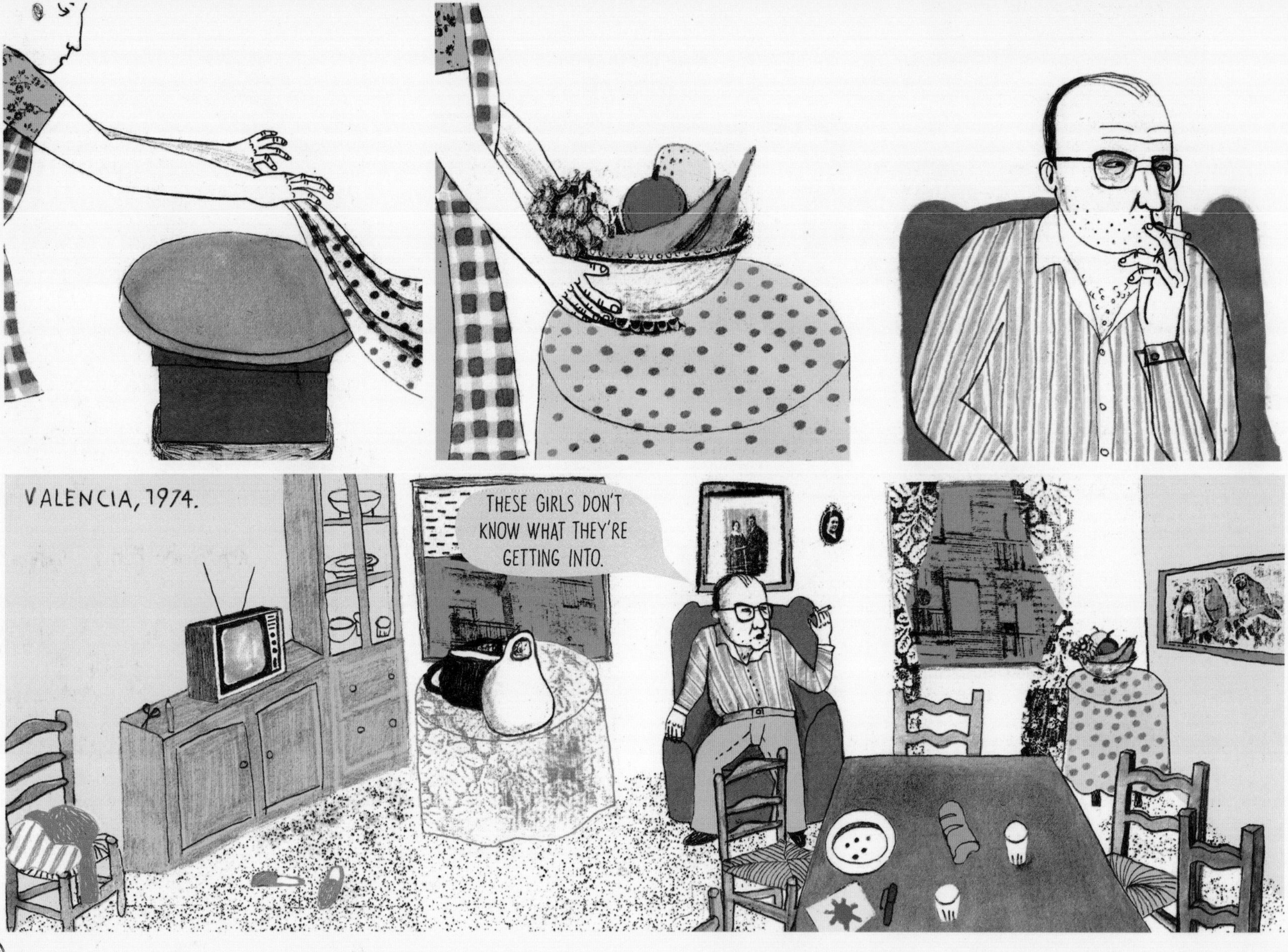
VALENCIA, 1974.
THESE GIRLS DON'T KNOW WHAT THEY'RE GETTING INTO.

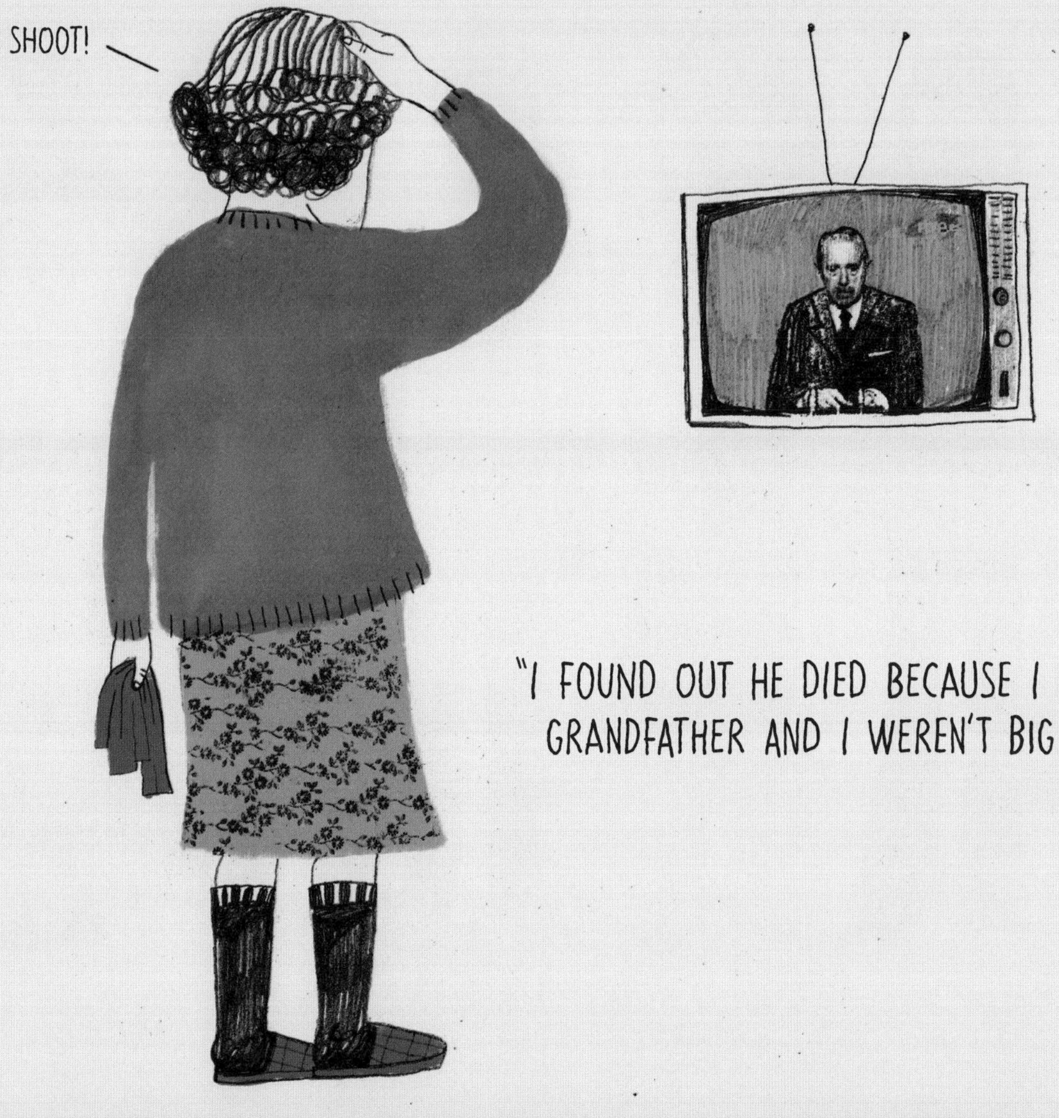
SHOOT!

"I FOUND OUT HE DIED BECAUSE I SAW IT ON TV. YOUR GRANDFATHER AND I WEREN'T BIG FANS OF FRANCO."

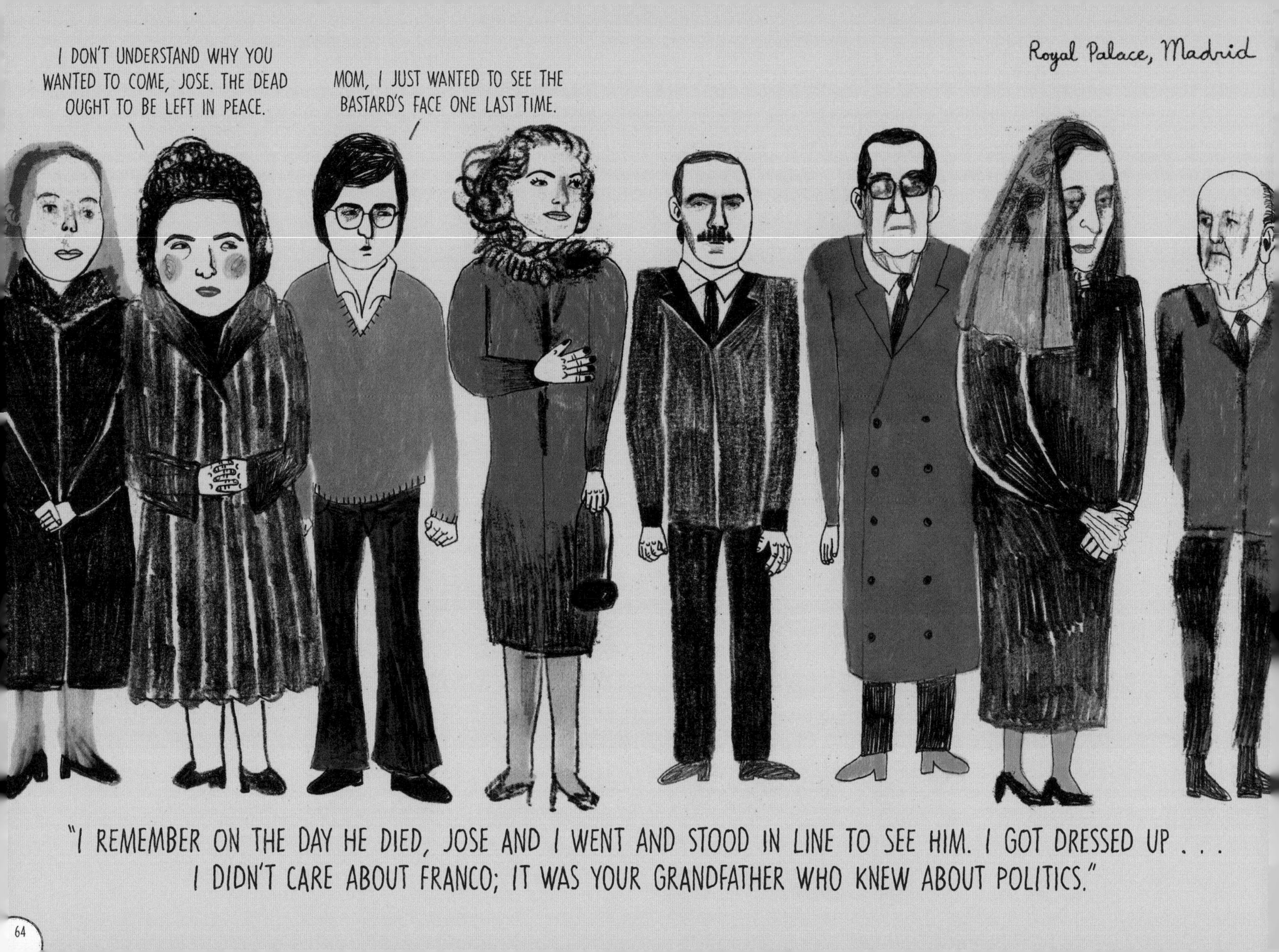
Royal Palace, Madrid
I DON'T UNDERSTAND WHY YOU WANTED TO COME, JOSE. THE DEAD OUGHT TO BE LEFT IN PEACE.
MOM, I JUST WANTED TO SEE THE BASTARD'S FACE ONE LAST TIME.
"I REMEMBER ON THE DAY HE DIED, JOSE AND I WENT AND STOOD IN LINE TO SEE HIM. I GOT DRESSED UP . . . I DIDN'T CARE ABOUT FRANCO; IT WAS YOUR GRANDFATHER WHO KNEW ABOUT POLITICS."

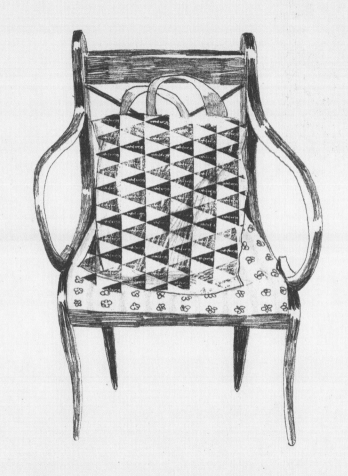

"THE BEST THING THAT'S HAPPENED TO ME IN LIFE IS DRIVING."

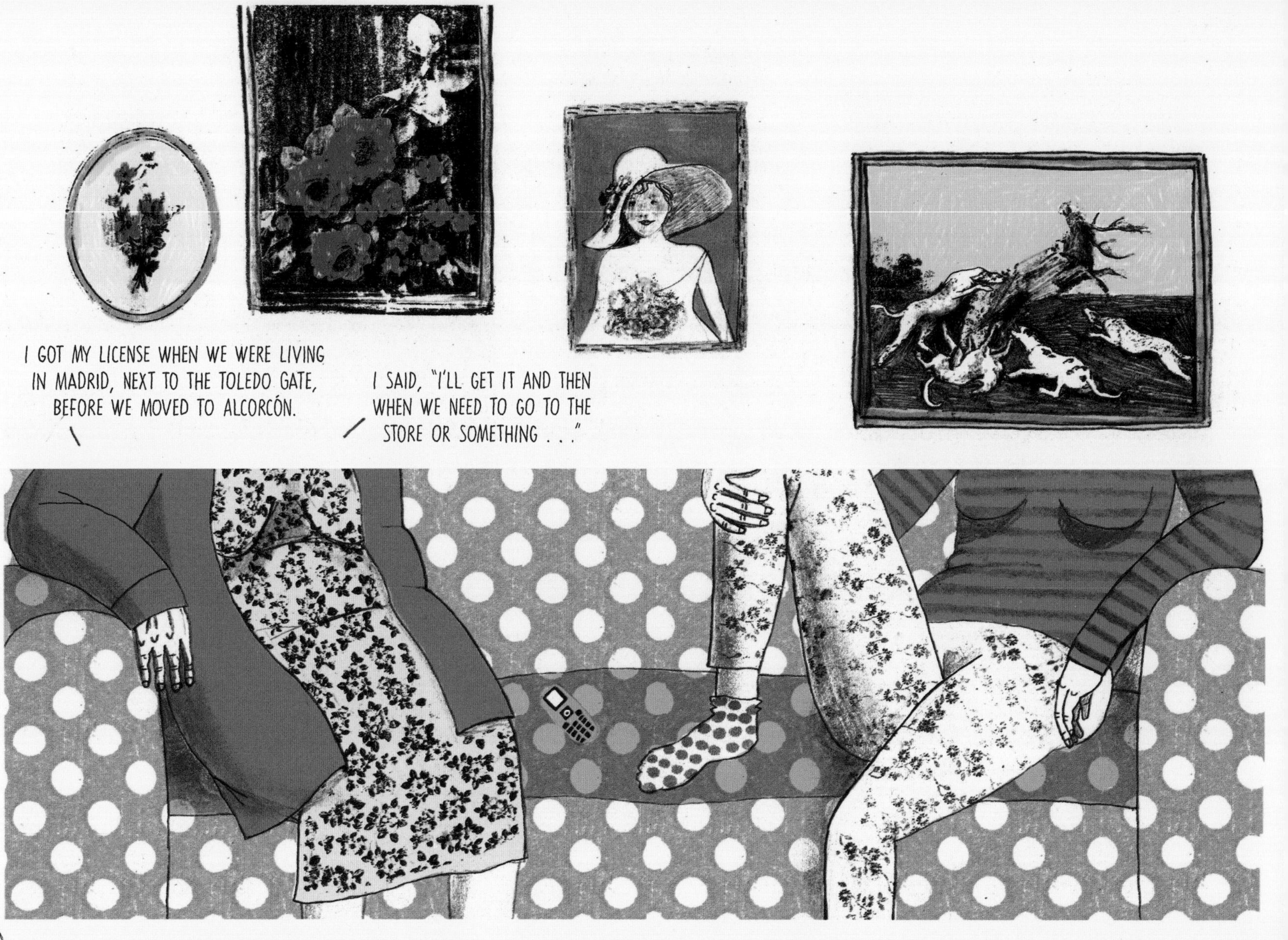
I GOT MY LICENSE WHEN WE WERE LIVING IN MADRID, NEXT TO THE TOLEDO GATE, BEFORE WE MOVED TO ALCORCÓN.
I SAID, "I'LL GET IT AND THEN WHEN WE NEED TO GO TO THE STORE OR SOMETHING . . ."

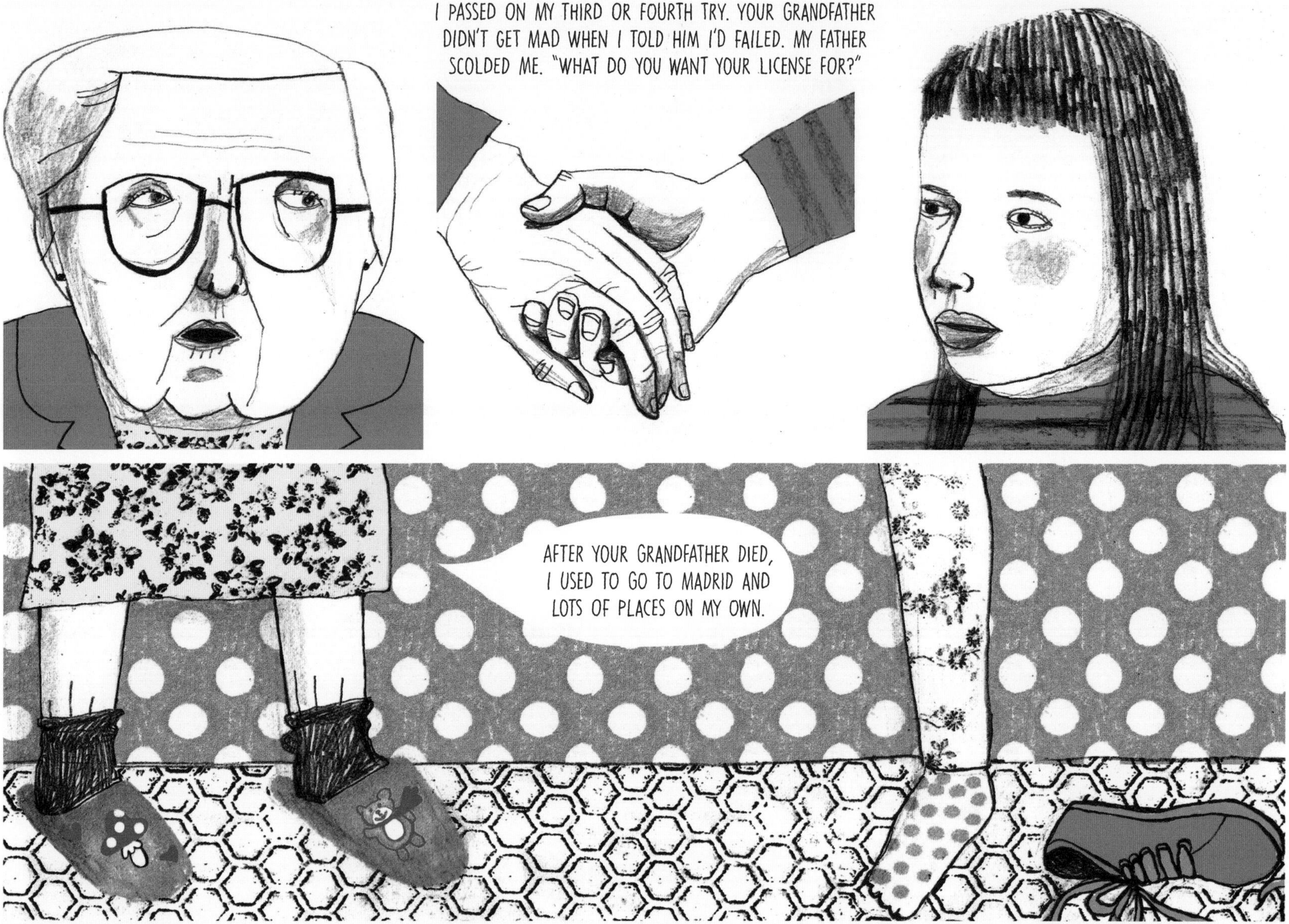
I PASSED ON MY THIRD OR FOURTH TRY. YOUR GRANDFATHER DIDN'T GET MAD WHEN I TOLD HIM I'D FAILED. MY FATHER SCOLDED ME. "WHAT DO YOU WANT YOUR LICENSE FOR?"
AFTER YOUR GRANDFATHER DIED, I USED TO GO TO MADRID AND LOTS OF PLACES ON MY OWN.

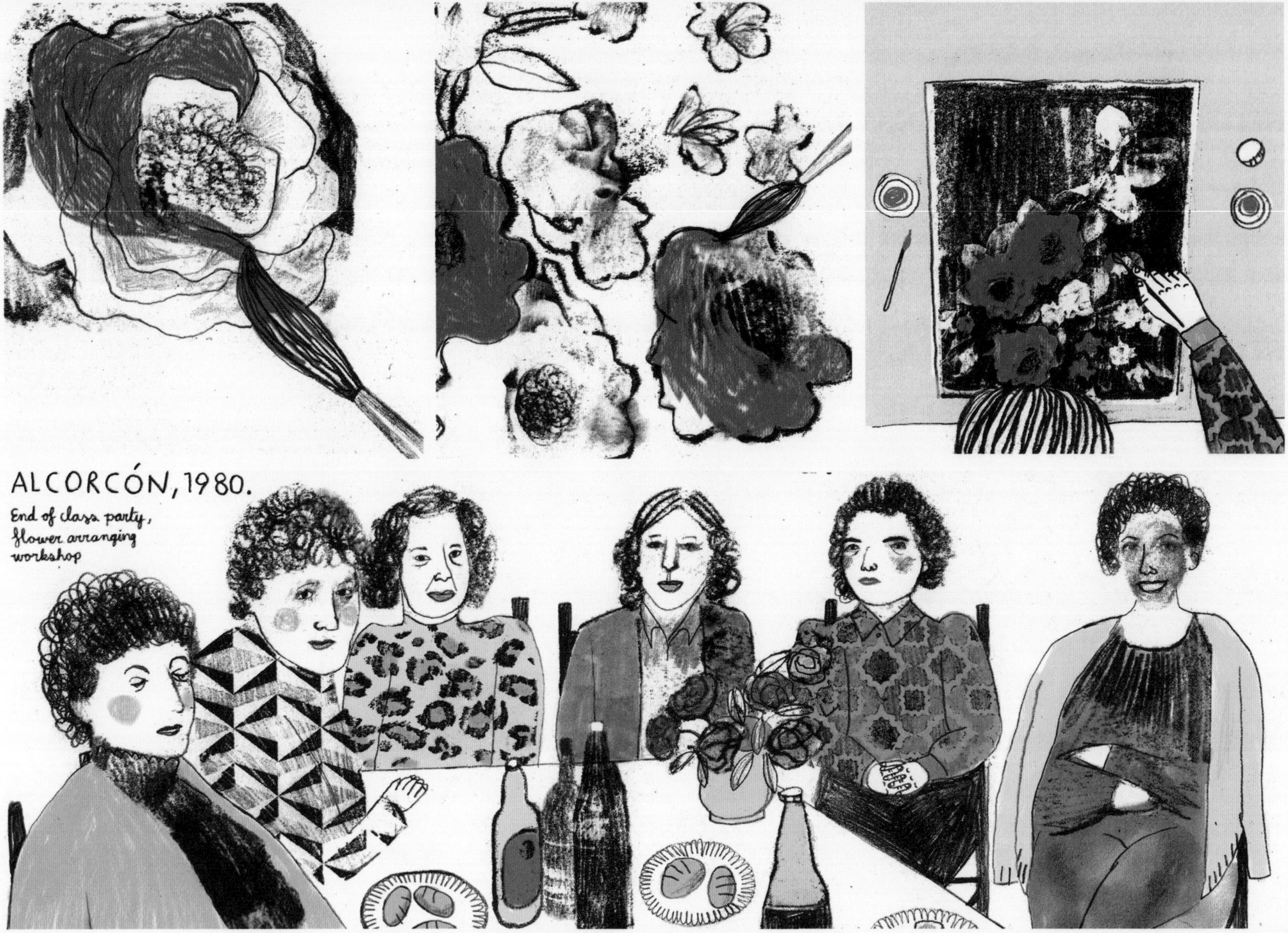
ALCORCÓN, 1980.
End of class party, flower arranging workshop

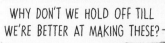

WHY DON'T WE HOLD OFF TILL WE'RE BETTER AT MAKING THESE?

NOTHING VENTURED, NOTHING GAINED, MARUJA!

ROSA, I'M SO NERVOUS MY STOMACH HURTS . . . YOU'RE WITH THE TIMES, BUT I'VE ALWAYS BEEN A STICK-IN-THE-MUD.

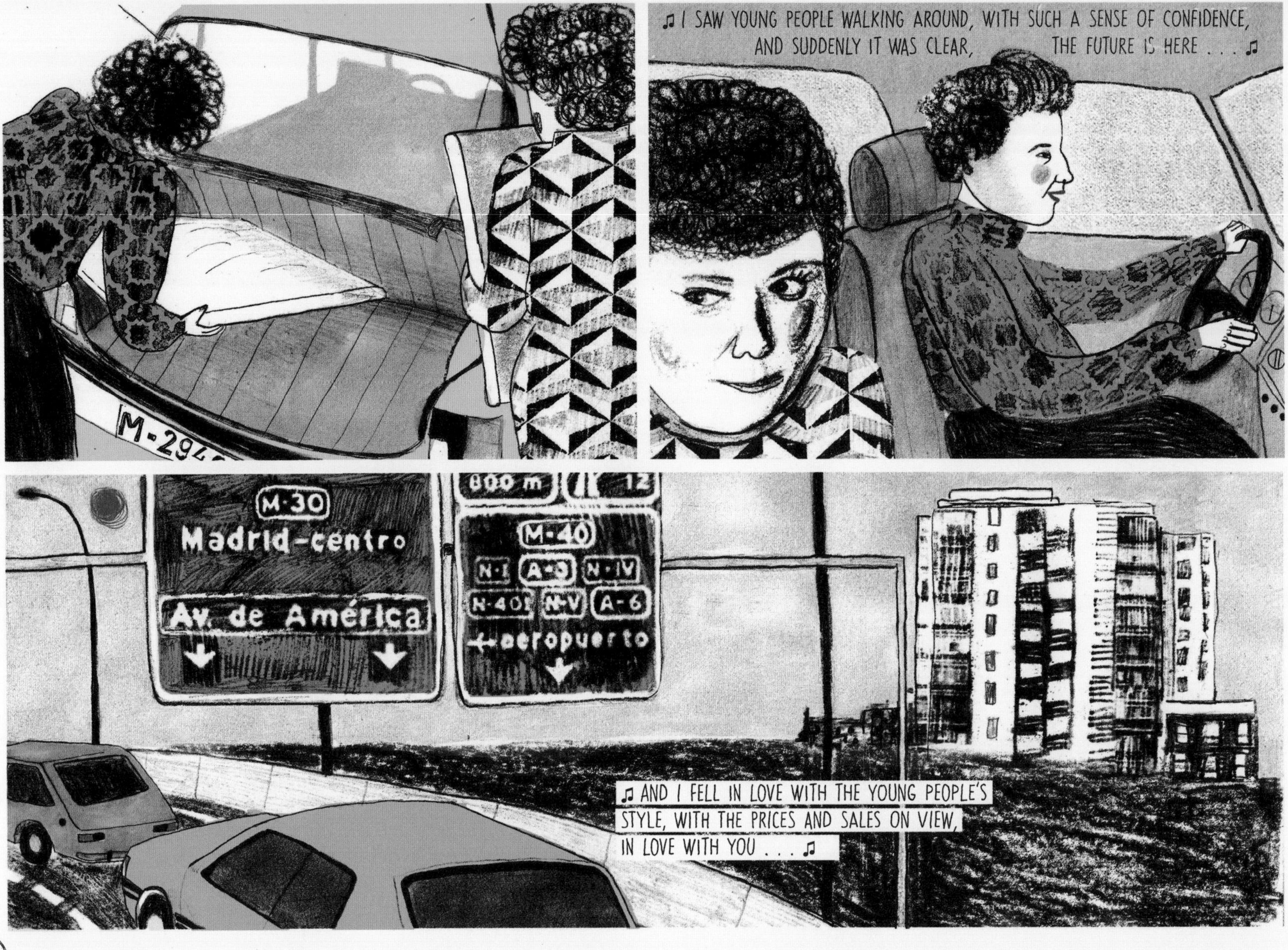
♫ I SAW YOUNG PEOPLE WALKING AROUND, WITH SUCH A SENSE OF CONFIDENCE, AND SUDDENLY IT WAS CLEAR, THE FUTURE IS HERE . . . ♫
800 m
12
M-30
Madrid-centro
Av. de América
M-40
N-I
N-IV
N-V
A-6
aeropuerto
♫ AND I FELL IN LOVE WITH THE YOUNG PEOPLE'S STYLE, WITH THE PRICES AND SALES ON VIEW, IN LOVE WITH YOU . . . ♫

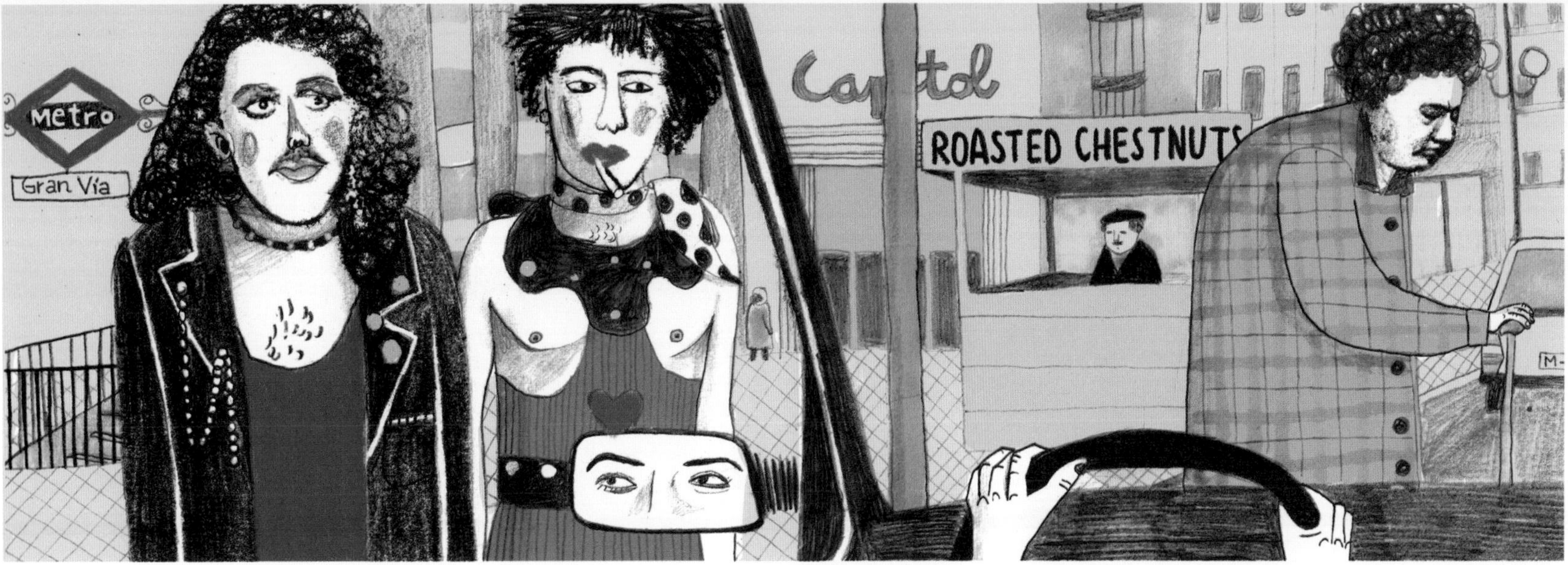
Metro
Gran Vía
ROASTED CHESTNUTS

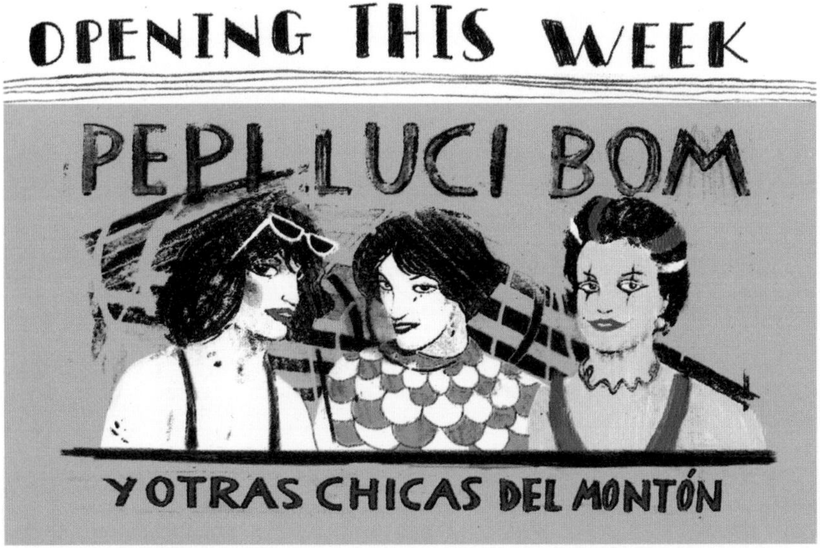
OPENING THIS WEEK
PEPI LUCI BOM
Y OTRAS CHICAS DEL MONTÓN

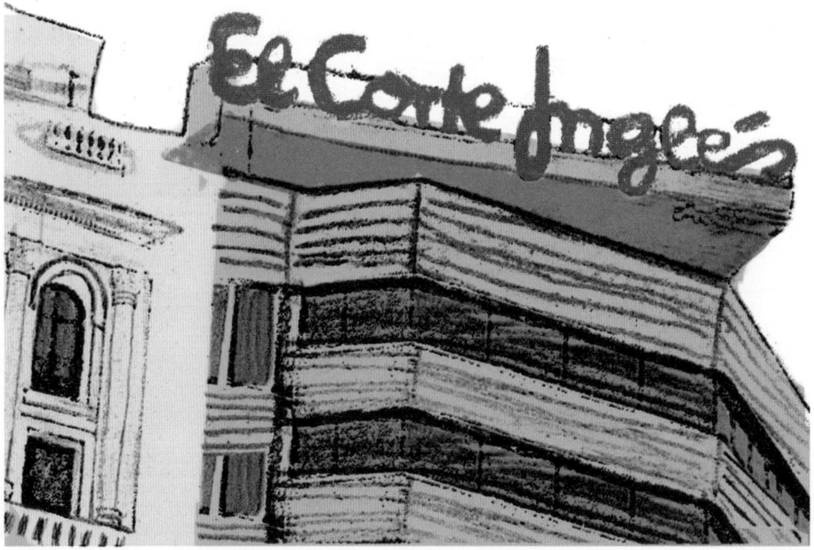
El Corte Inglés

YOU MAKE ME HOT, HANDSOME . . .
COULD YOU MAKE ME TEN MORE FOR NEXT MONTH?
OF COURSE.

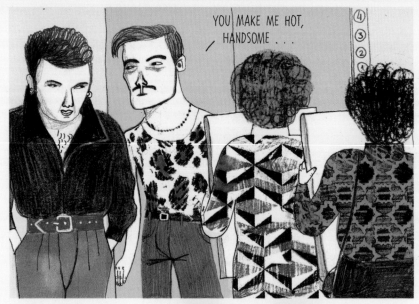

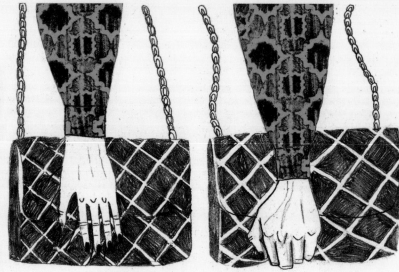

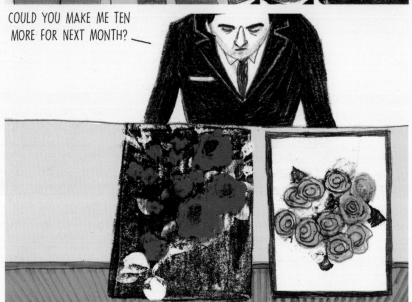

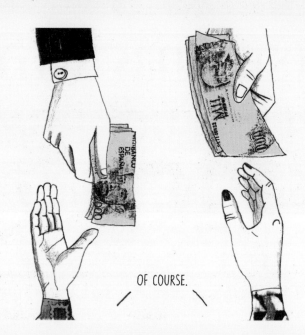

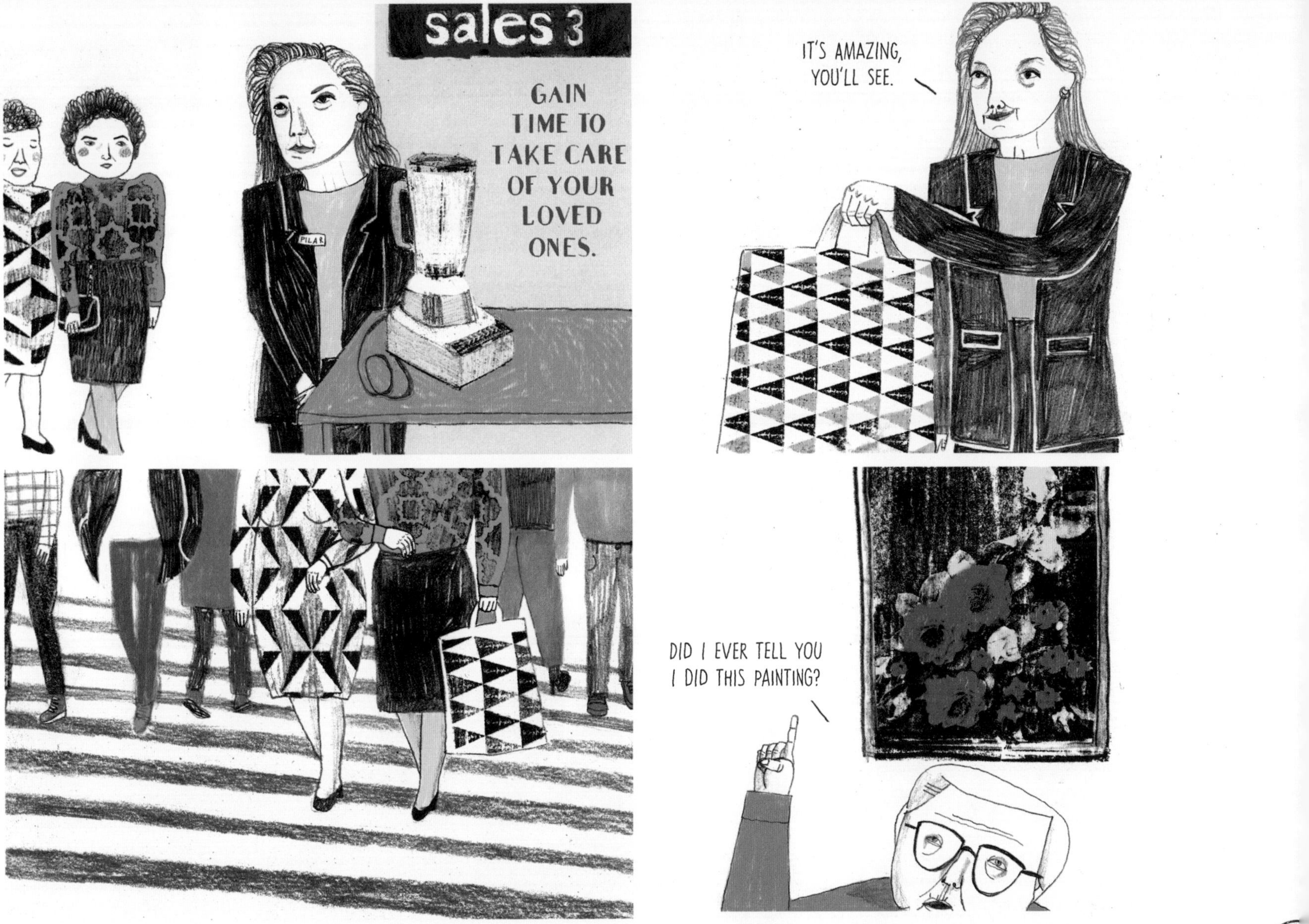
sales 3
PILAR
GAIN TIME TO TAKE CARE OF YOUR LOVED ONES.
IT'S AMAZING, YOU'LL SEE.
DID I EVER TELL YOU I DID THIS PAINTING?

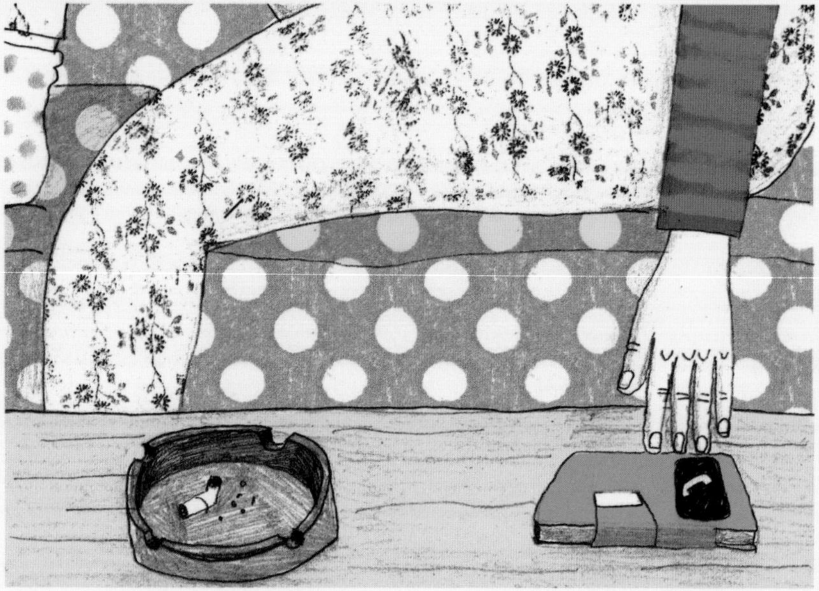

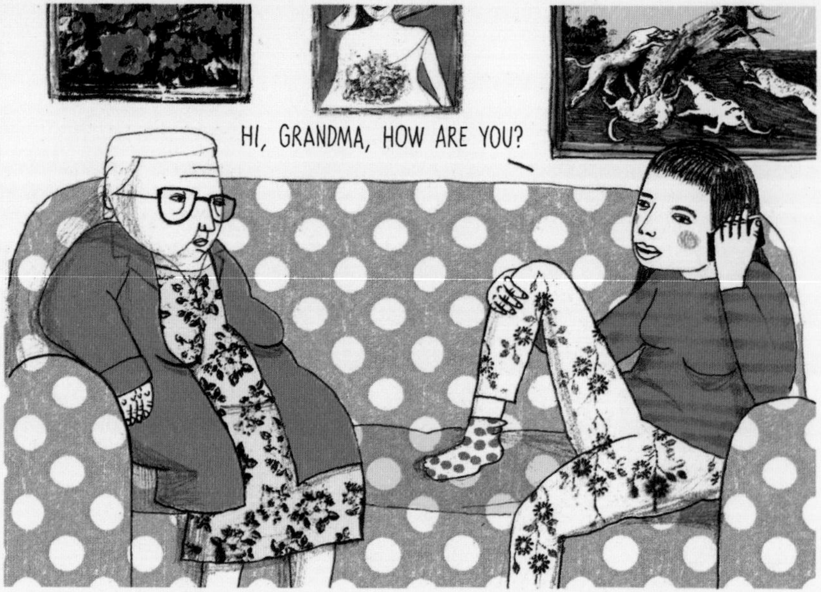
HI, GRANDMA, HOW ARE YOU?

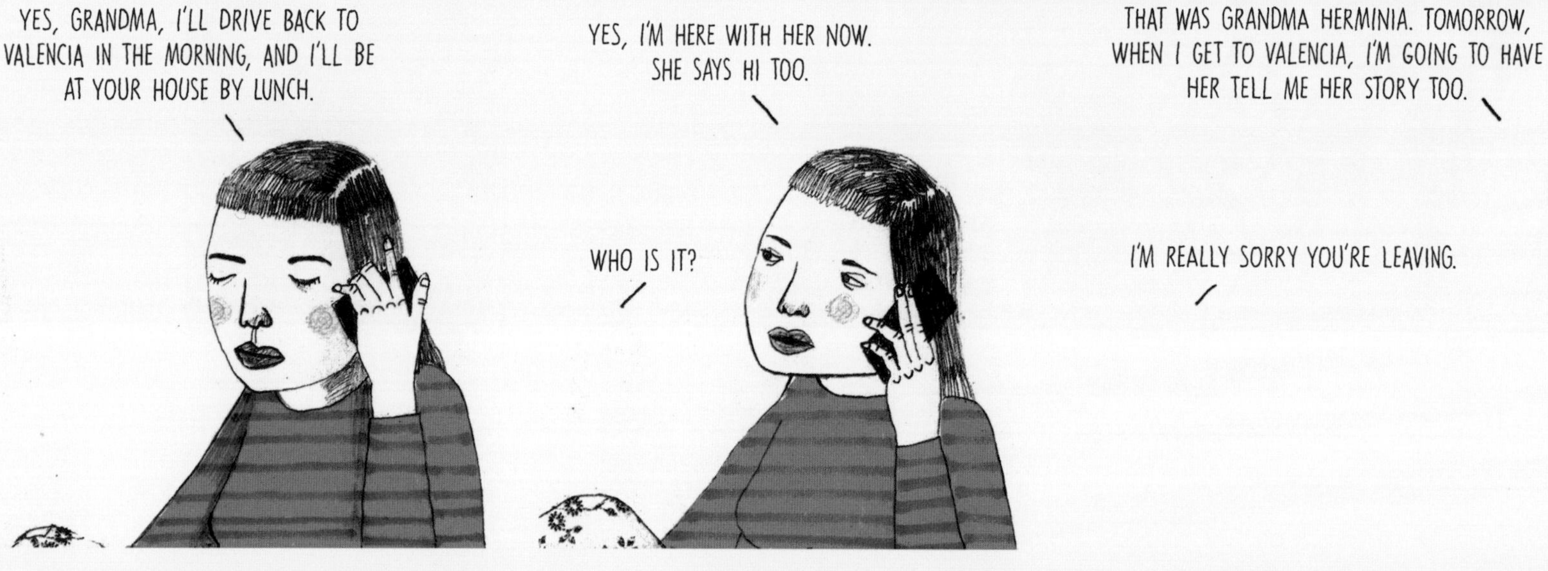
YES, GRANDMA, I'LL DRIVE BACK TO VALENCIA IN THE MORNING, AND I'LL BE AT YOUR HOUSE BY LUNCH.
YES, I'M HERE WITH HER NOW. SHE SAYS HI TOO.
WHO IS IT?
THAT WAS GRANDMA HERMINIA. TOMORROW, WHEN I GET TO VALENCIA, I'M GOING TO HAVE HER TELL ME HER STORY TOO.
I'M REALLY SORRY YOU'RE LEAVING.

"I REMEMBER WHENEVER I WENT TO THE STORE, ALFONSO USED TO SAY,
'I'VE NEVER SEEN A WOMAN DO THE SHOPPING IN SLIPPERS AND SOCKS.'
YES, I WAS REALLY OVERWHELMED."

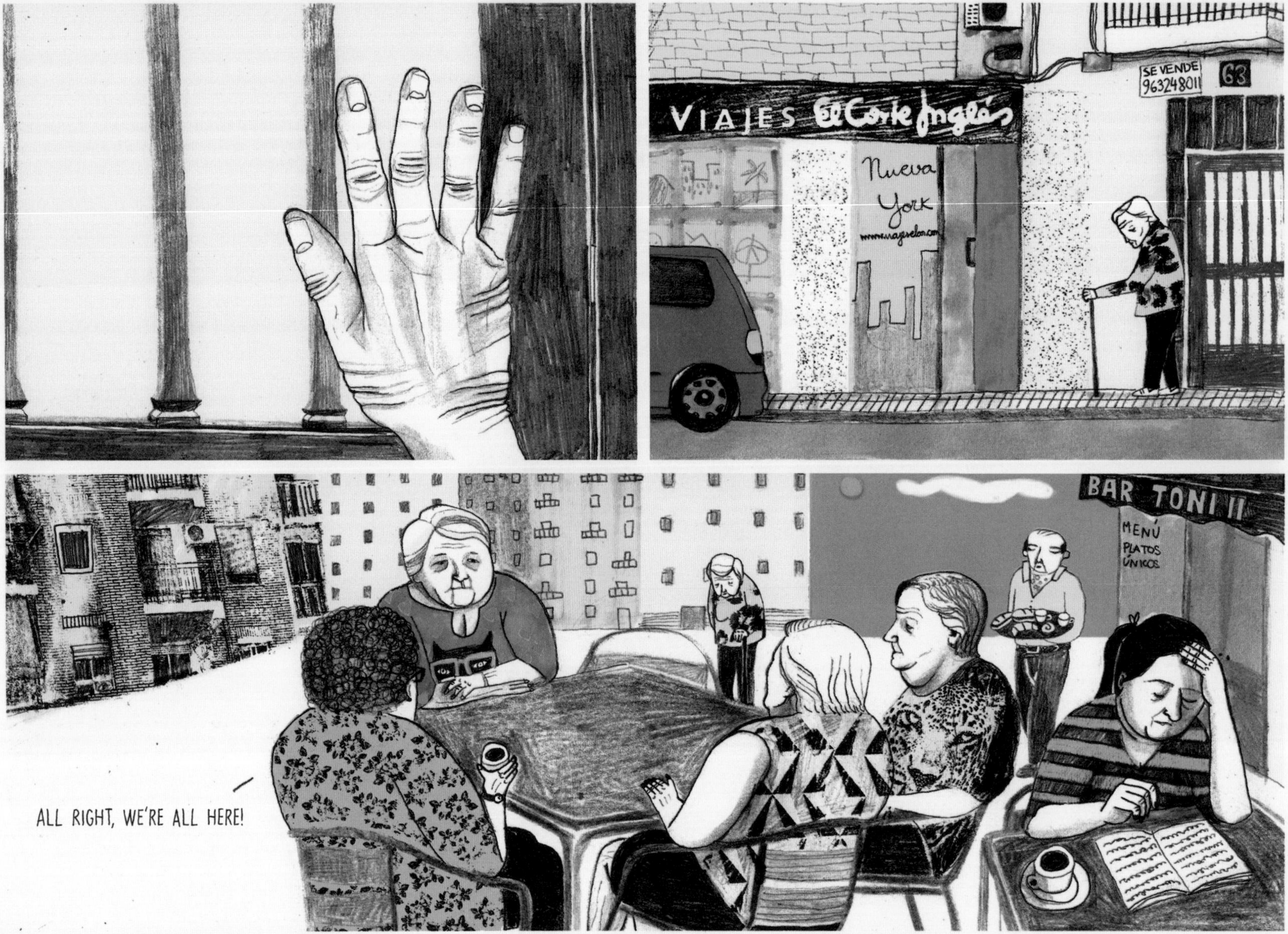

VIAJES El Corte Inglés
Nueva York
SE VENDE 963248011
63
BAR TONI II
MENÚ PLATOS ÚNICOS
ALL RIGHT, WE'RE ALL HERE!

HOW ARE THE MEDS, HERMINIA?

I THINK MY BLOOD PRESSURE'S UP AGAIN.

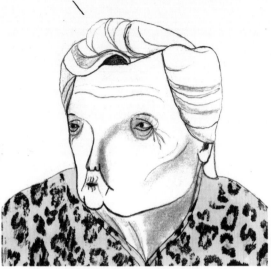

I HAVEN'T SLEPT A WINK.

MY LEGS GET WORSE EVERY DAY.

I HAVEN'T GONE TO THE BATHROOM TODAY EITHER.

WE'RE A TOTAL MESS!

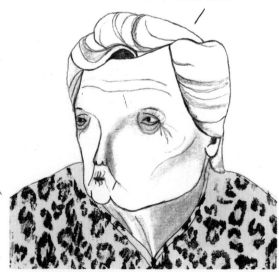

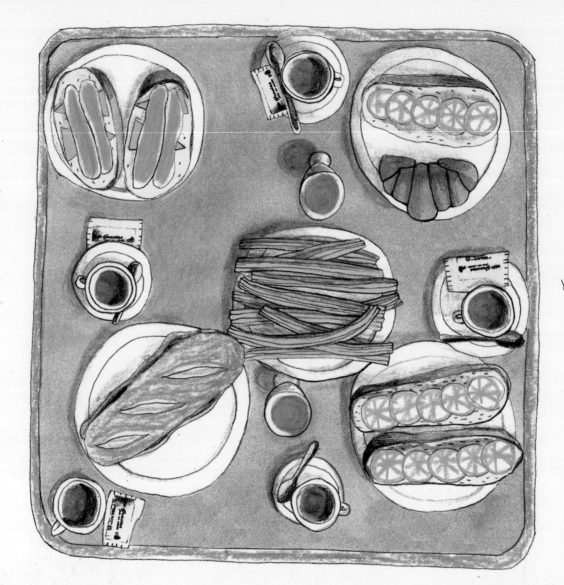

YOU LADIES DON'T SHOUT,
YOU BLEAT!

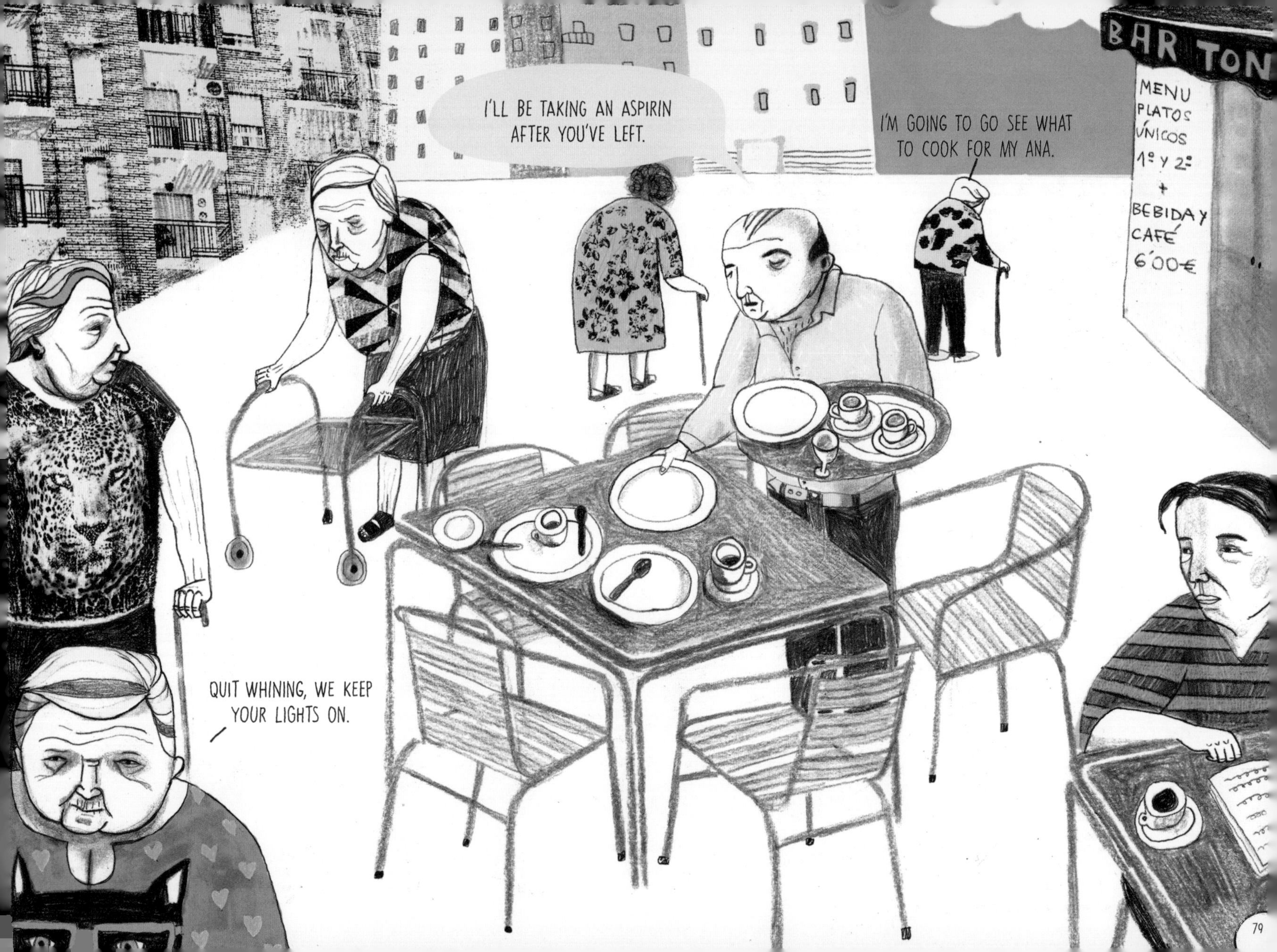
BAR TON
I'LL BE TAKING AN ASPIRIN AFTER YOU'VE LEFT.
I'M GOING TO GO SEE WHAT TO COOK FOR MY ANA.
MENU PLATOS ÚNICOS 1º Y 2º + BEBIDA Y CAFÉ 6'00€
QUIT WHINING, WE KEEP YOUR LIGHTS ON.

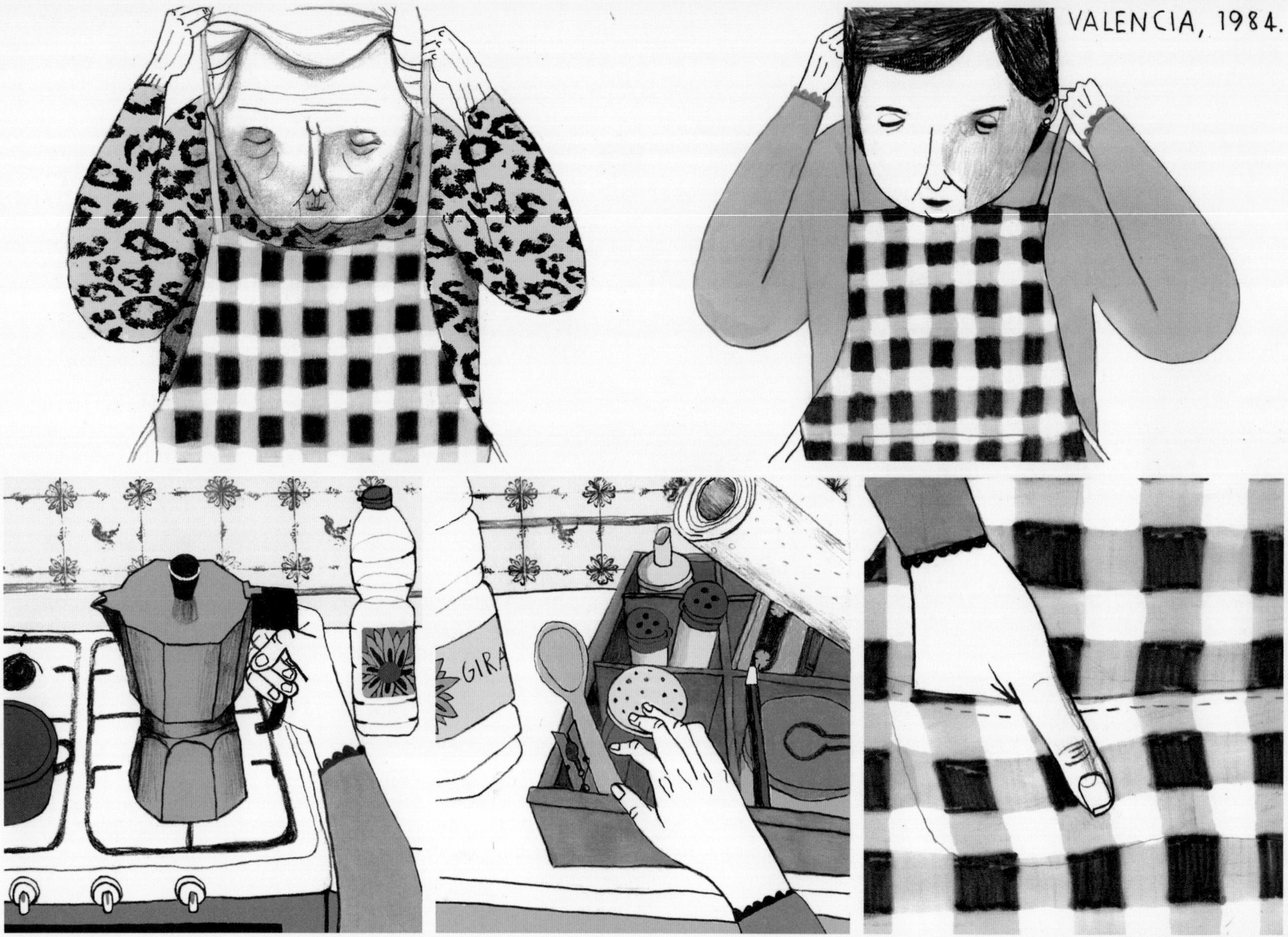
VALENCIA, 1984.
GIRA

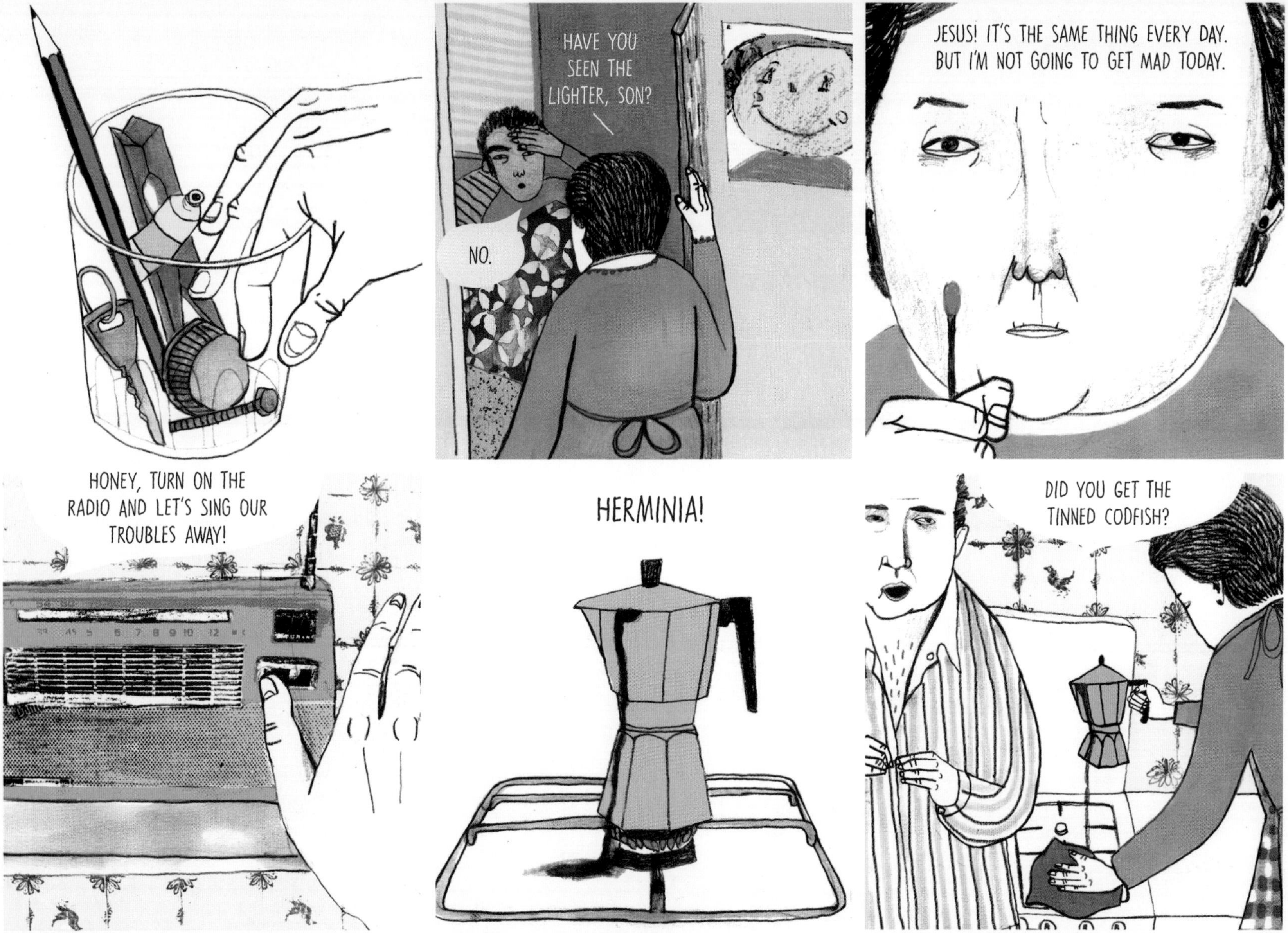
HAVE YOU SEEN THE LIGHTER, SON?
NO.
JESUS! IT'S THE SAME THING EVERY DAY. BUT I'M NOT GOING TO GET MAD TODAY.
HONEY, TURN ON THE RADIO AND LET'S SING OUR TROUBLES AWAY!
HERMINIA!
DID YOU GET THE TINNED CODFISH?

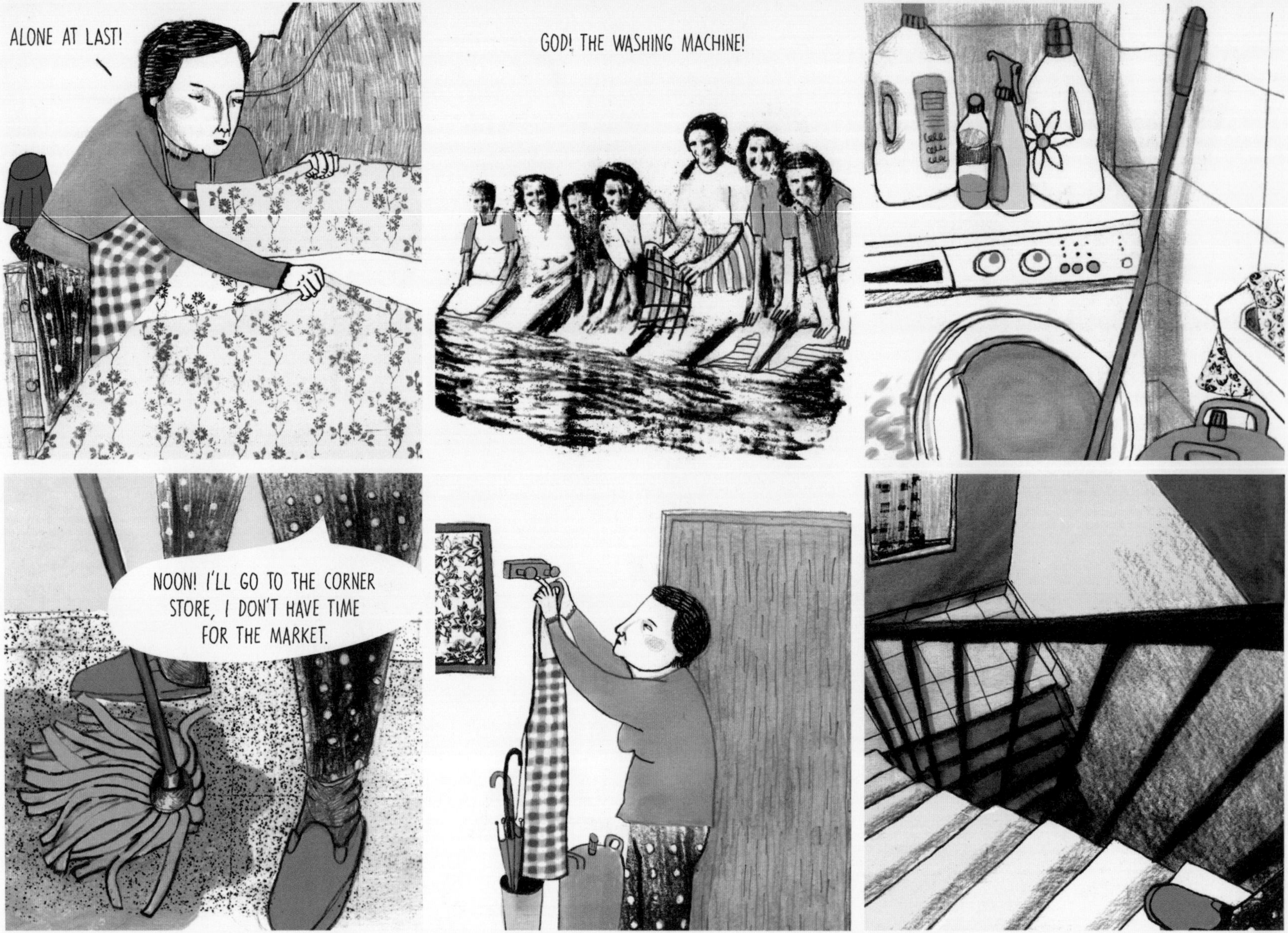
ALONE AT LAST!
GOD! THE WASHING MACHINE!
NOON! I'LL GO TO THE CORNER STORE, I DON'T HAVE TIME FOR THE MARKET.

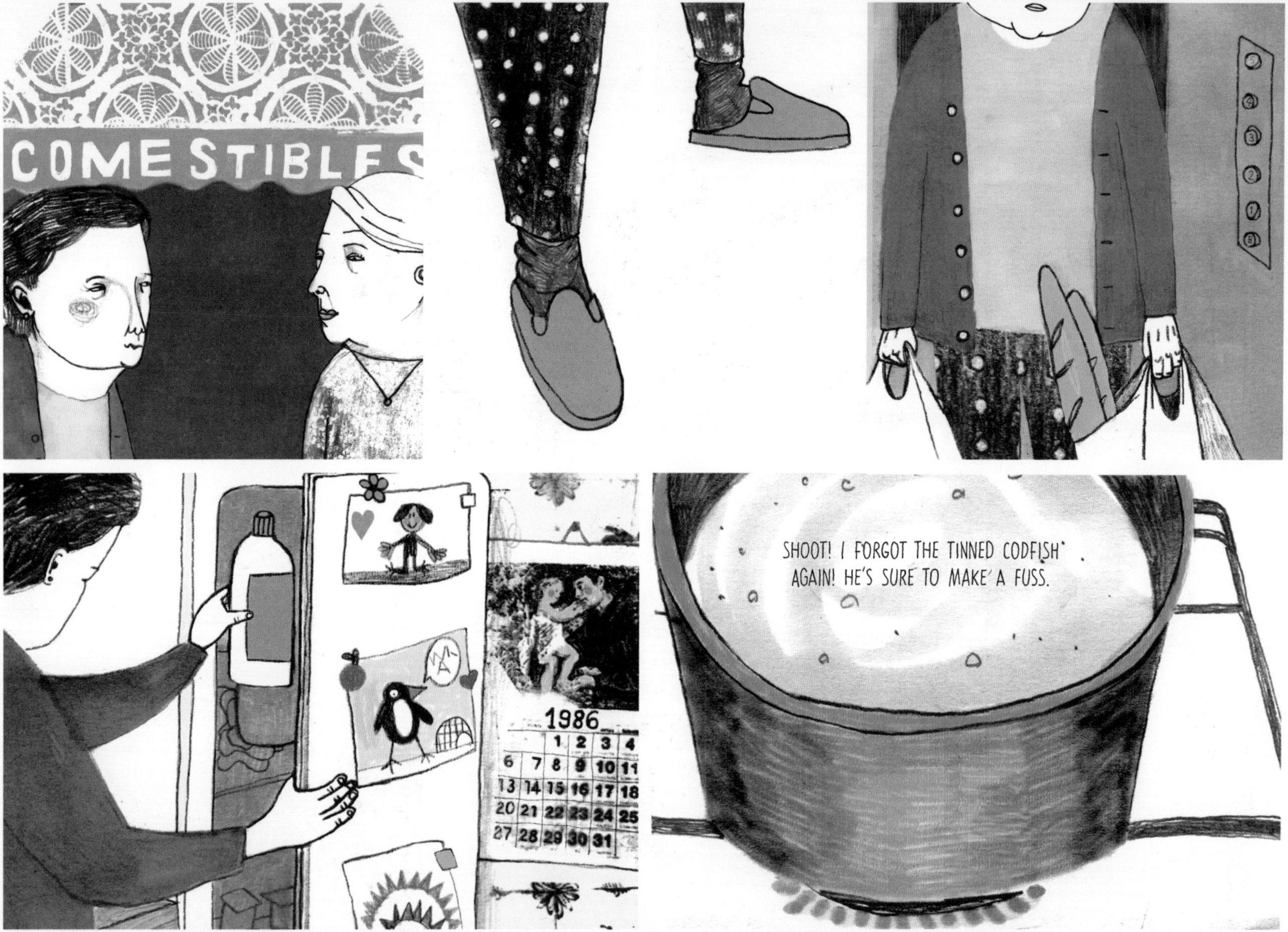
COMESTIBLES
1986
SHOOT! I FORGOT THE TINNED CODFISH AGAIN! HE'S SURE TO MAKE A FUSS.

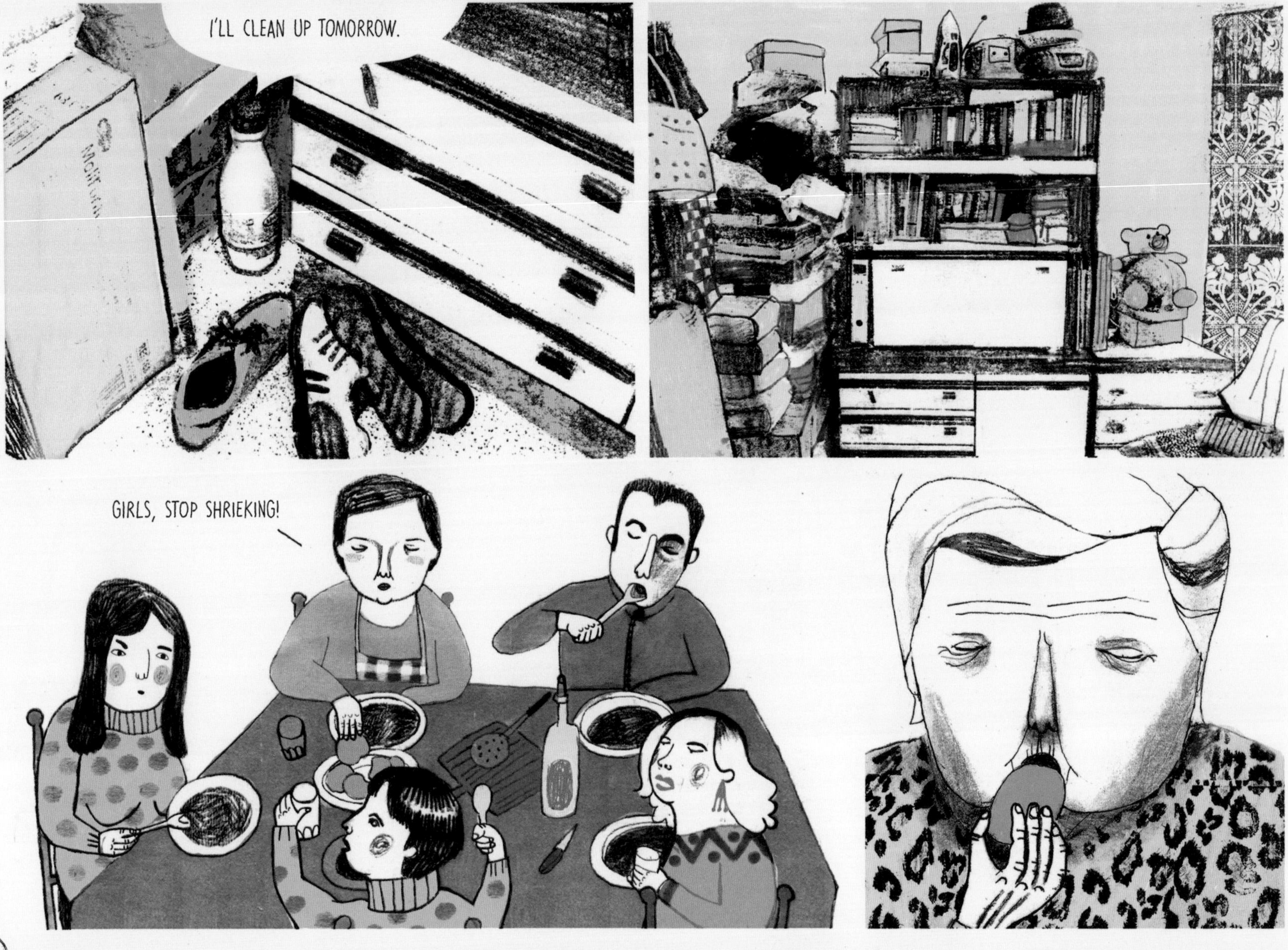
I'LL CLEAN UP TOMORROW.
GIRLS, STOP SHRIEKING!

WELL, I DIDN'T FIND THE HOUSE AND CHILDREN TO BE MUCH WORK. WANT TO KNOW SOMETHING ELSE?

REST, GRANDMA. WE'VE BEEN TALKING FOR THREE HOURS! IF YOU WANT, WE CAN KEEP GOING LATER, WHILE WE LOOK AT THE PHOTOS.

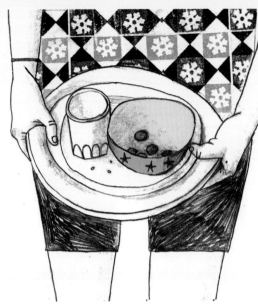

GRANDMA, AT LEAST LET ME DO THE DISHES!

NOT A CHANCE! JUST LEAVE THE SKILLET TO SOAK. AND BRING THE WHISKEY, HONEY. I'LL POUR A LITTLE IN MY COFFEE.

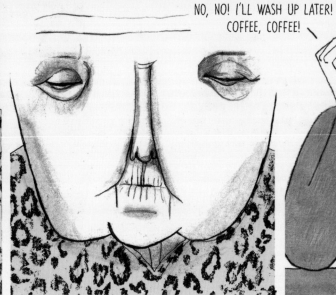

NO, NO! I'LL WASH UP LATER! COFFEE, COFFEE!

FIVE O'CLOCK! I PROMISED GLORIA I'D PICK THE KIDS UP FROM SCHOOL.

THE BEDS! THAT'S OK, WE'LL BE GOING TO BED SOON ANYWAY.

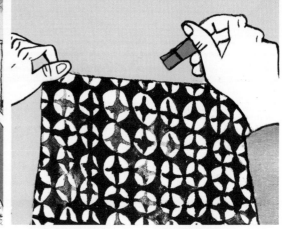

IT'S WONDERFUL YOU'VE COME TO VISIT, SON. I DON'T GET TO SEE MUCH OF YOU!

GOODNESS, THERE'S BASKETBALL ON!

MOM, DID YOU CALL THE REPAIRMAN?

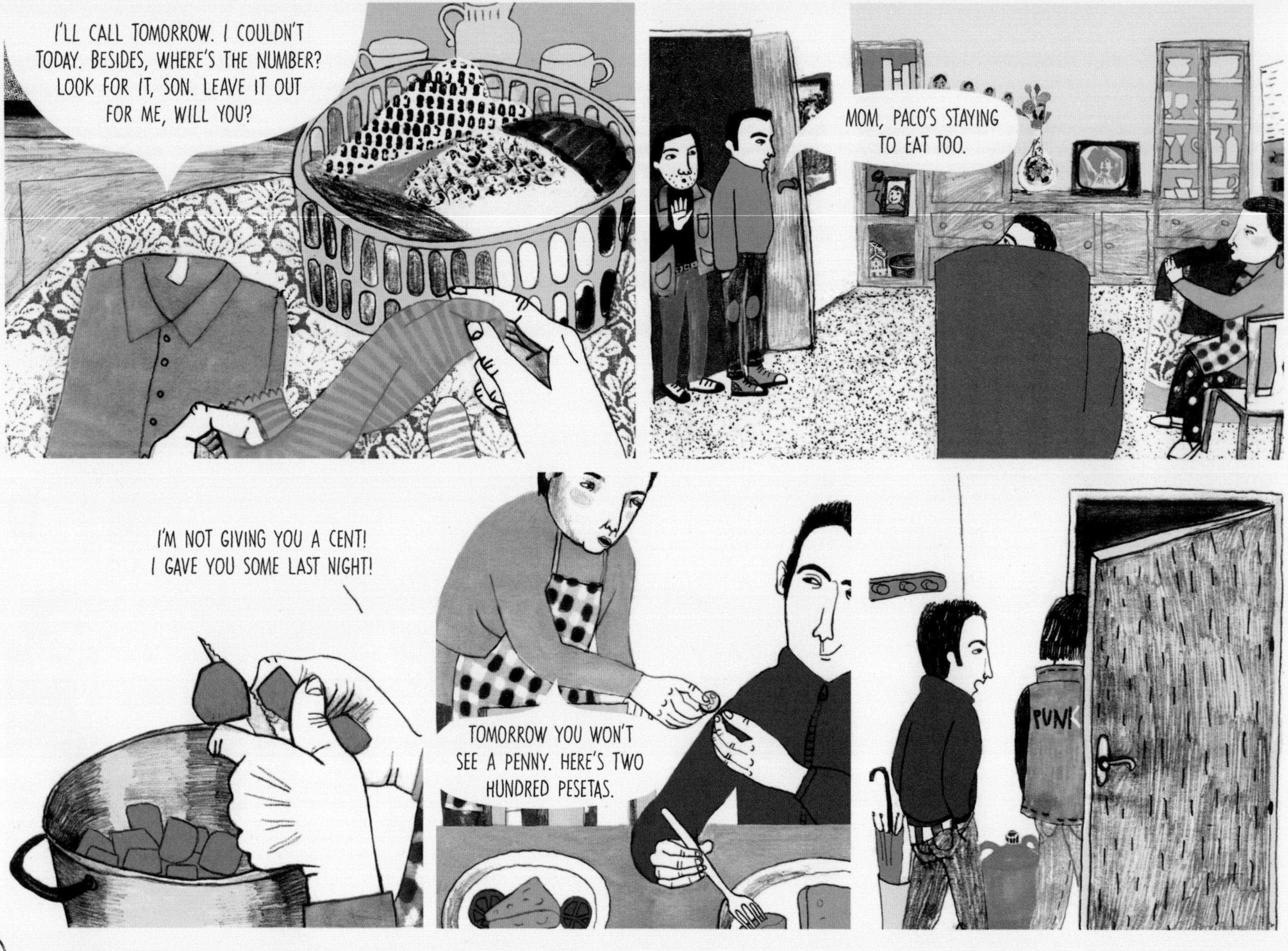
I'LL CALL TOMORROW. I COULDN'T TODAY. BESIDES, WHERE'S THE NUMBER? LOOK FOR IT, SON. LEAVE IT OUT FOR ME, WILL YOU?
MOM, PACO'S STAYING TO EAT TOO.
I'M NOT GIVING YOU A CENT! I GAVE YOU SOME LAST NIGHT!
TOMORROW YOU WON'T SEE A PENNY. HERE'S TWO HUNDRED PESETAS.
PUNK

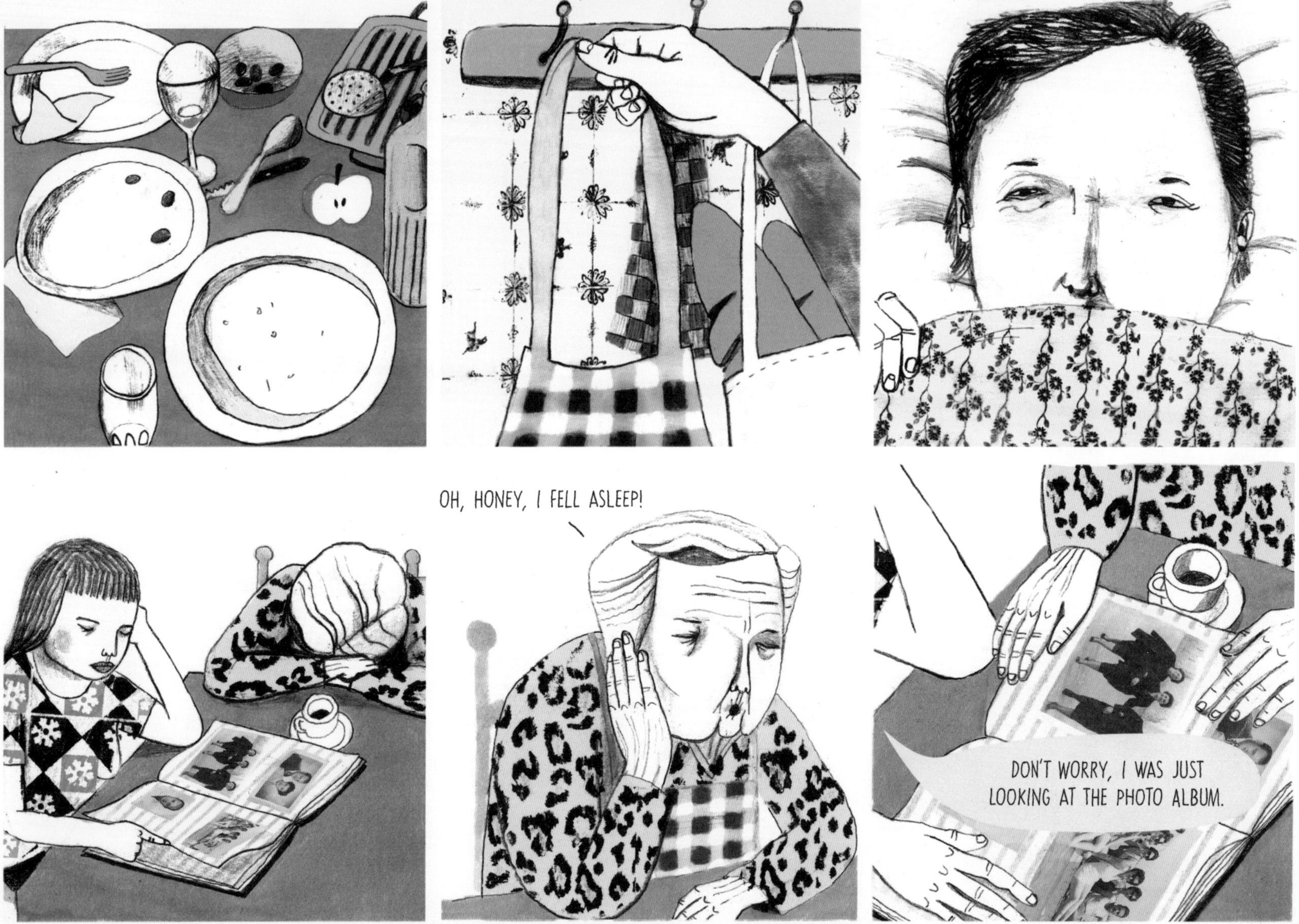
OH, HONEY, I FELL ASLEEP!
DON'T WORRY, I WAS JUST LOOKING AT THE PHOTO ALBUM.

THIS IS MY GRANDFATHER JUAN ALONSO. HE DIED WHEN MY MOTHER LEFT BECAUSE HE WAS SO DISTRAUGHT.

HE WAS THE ONE WHO RAN THE TOWN THEATER. OUR HOME WAS CONNECTED TO THE THEATER; IT WASN'T YOUR AVERAGE HOUSE. THERE WERE LOTS OF DOORS, AND PEOPLE WERE CONSTANTLY COMING AND GOING: ARTISTS, NEIGHBORS . . . THERE WAS A LOT OF ATMOSPHERE.

IS IT TRUE SHE GOT CHASED BY A MOB WITH CLUBS?

I DIDN'T SEE THAT, I JUST HEARD ABOUT IT.

AND THIS IS MY MOTHER, MAY SHE REST IN PEACE.

HOW DID THE STORY GO?

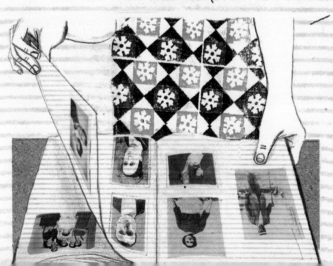

MY GRANDFATHER BOUGHT AN INN IN ALBACETE AND TOOK MY MOTHER THERE TO WORK; MY FATHER STAYED IN TOWN TO RUN THE THEATER.

IN ALBACETE, MY MOTHER MET A MAN WHO WAS A FRUIT VENDOR. JOAQUÍN VIVO. MY MOTHER ALREADY HAD SIX CHILDREN AND JOAQUÍN WAS A BACHELOR, THE POLAR OPPOSITE OF MY FATHER, WHO WASN'T A HARD WORKER.

AND THAT MAN MUST HAVE SAID SOMETHING TO HER, BECAUSE MY MOTHER WAS A GOOD-LOOKING WOMAN BACK THEN, SHE HAD A SPECIAL SORT OF GRACE. BECAUSE SHE KNEW THE THEATER, HAD DEALT WITH ARTISTS, SHE HAD A DIFFERENT MIND-SET. AND LITTLE BY LITTLE, THAT MAN WON HER OVER.

LATER SHE CAME BACK TO TOWN TO END THE RELATIONSHIP AND STAY WITH US. BUT THE MAN KEPT WRITING TO HER—HE WAS IN LOVE WITH HER. AND SHE WAS IN LOVE WITH HIM. MADLY IN LOVE.

AND ONE DAY A LITTLE BOY CAME LOOKING FOR MY MOTHER WITH A NOTE SAYING THAT JOAQUÍN VIVO WAS WAITING FOR HER IN HIS CAR. AND APPARENTLY COUSIN ISABEL, WHO LIVED IN THE HOUSE, SAW MY MOTHER BUNDLE HER MOST CHERISHED POSSESSIONS INTO A PIECE OF CLOTH. AND SINCE THERE WERE ALREADY RUMORS, SHE REALIZED MY MOTHER WAS TAKING OFF.

AND AS MY MOTHER WAS GOING DOWN THE STAIRS, COUSIN ISABEL STARTED YELLING: "MY COUSIN'S LEAVING, MY COUSIN'S LEAVING!"

AND SEVERAL MEN APPEARED, ONE WITH A GARROTE, ONE WITH A CLUB, AND WENT AFTER HER. JOAQUÍN WAS WAITING FOR HER ON THE CORNER NEXT TO ISABEL DE GRILLO'S HOUSE. THEY ALMOST CAUGHT HER AS SHE WAS CLIMBING INTO THE CAR.

IF THEY'D CAUGHT HER JUST THEN, THEY'D HAVE KILLED HER! THAT'S WHY MY MOTHER HAD A LOT OF FAITH IN THE VIRGIN OF CONSOLATION. AND SHE TOOK OFF FOR ALBACETE. MY GRANDFATHER WAS SHATTERED. WHAT I DON'T KNOW IS WHEN MY MOTHER LEFT. I KNOW IT WAS BEFORE THE WAR. I WOULD HAVE BEEN FOUR YEARS OLD.

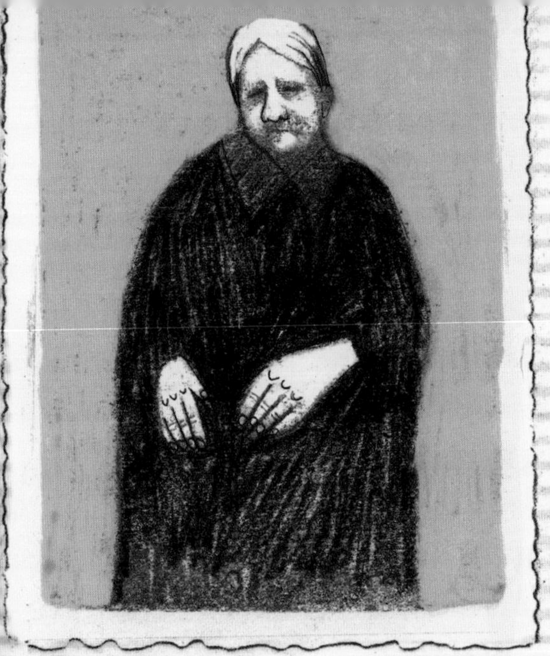

I WAS WELL TAKEN CARE OF BY MY GRANDMOTHER. SHE WAS THE ONE WHO GAVE ME BREAKFAST; SHE LOOKED AFTER ME MORE THAN MY MOTHER DID.

MY GRANDMOTHER WAS THE ONE WHO TOLD ME STORIES, THE ONES I LATER TOLD TO YOU WHEN YOU WERE LITTLE. GRANDMA HERMENEGILDA KNEW HOW TO READ, WHICH WASN'T ALL THAT COMMON FOR WOMEN BACK THEN! THERE WAS A LITTLE LIBRARY AT THE THEATER THAT HAD THE "ONE THOUSAND AND ONE NIGHTS," AND MY GRANDMOTHER WOULD READ IT TO ME BEFORE I WENT TO SLEEP.

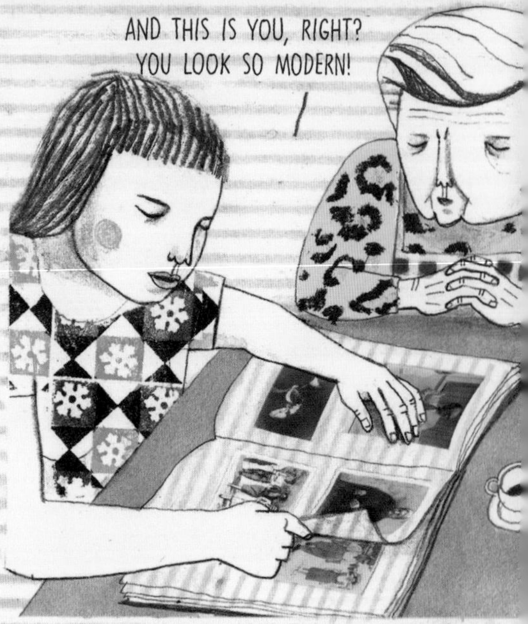
AND THIS IS YOU, RIGHT? YOU LOOK SO MODERN!

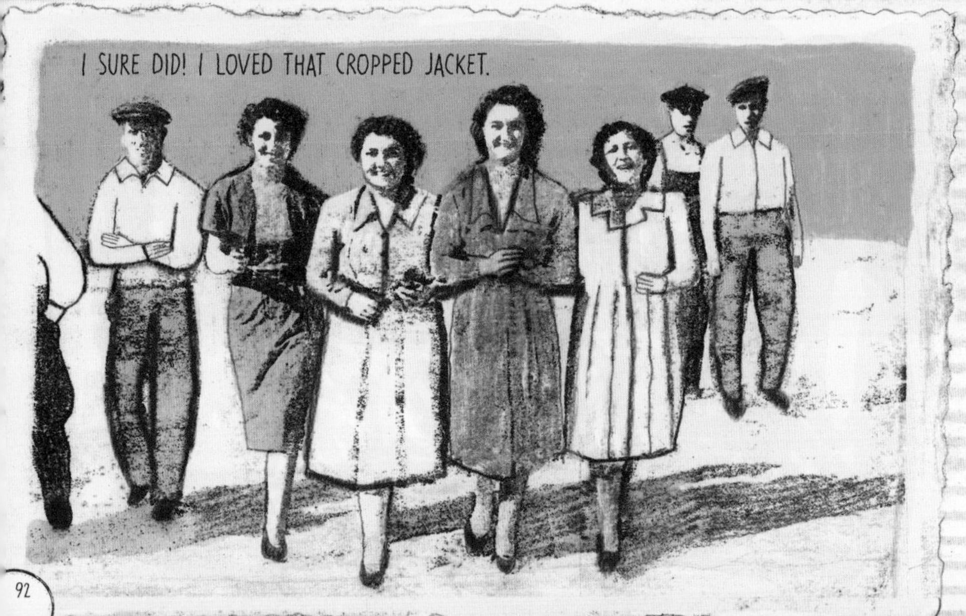
I SURE DID! I LOVED THAT CROPPED JACKET.

AND HERE I AM WITH YOUR GRANDFATHER AT THE DANCE. YOU MIGHT NOT GUESS IT, BUT AS A YOUNG MAN, HE WAS QUITE THE ROMANTIC!

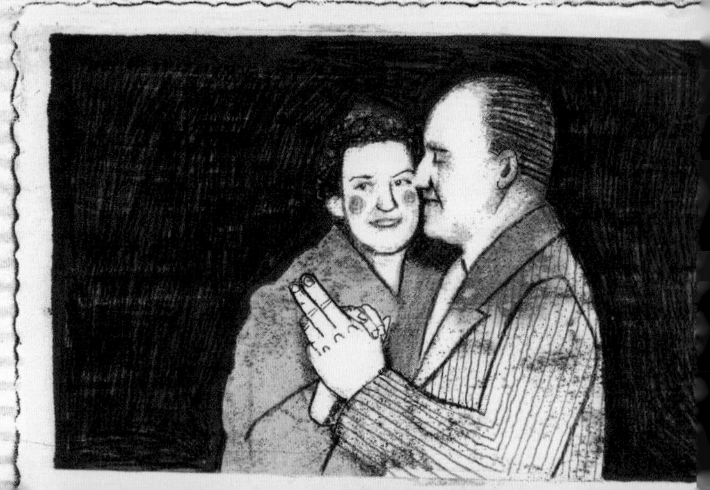

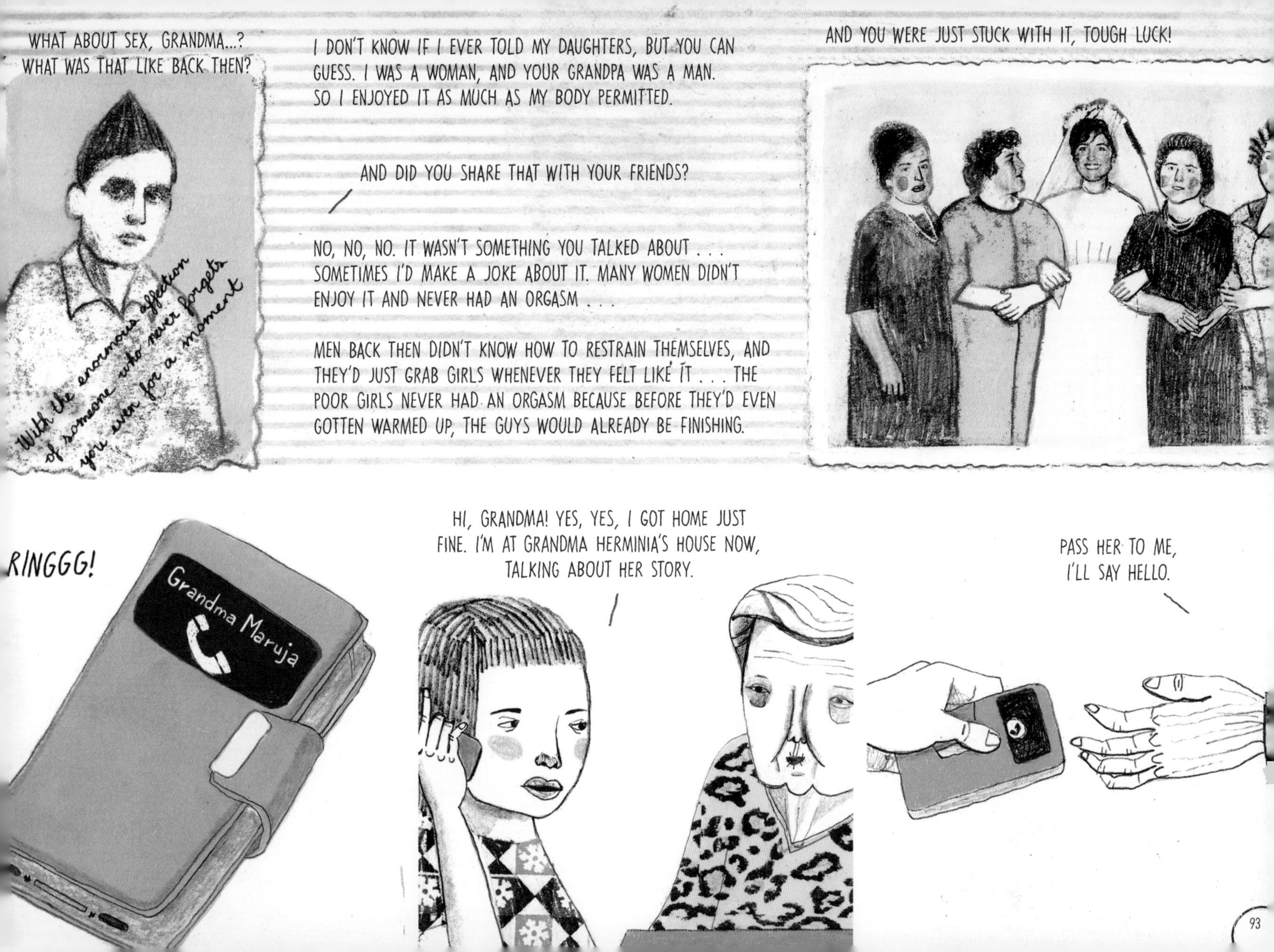
WHAT ABOUT SEX, GRANDMA...? WHAT WAS THAT LIKE BACK THEN?
With the enormous affection of someone who never forgets you even for a moment
I DON'T KNOW IF I EVER TOLD MY DAUGHTERS, BUT YOU CAN GUESS. I WAS A WOMAN, AND YOUR GRANDPA WAS A MAN. SO I ENJOYED IT AS MUCH AS MY BODY PERMITTED.
AND DID YOU SHARE THAT WITH YOUR FRIENDS?
NO, NO, NO. IT WASN'T SOMETHING YOU TALKED ABOUT . . . SOMETIMES I'D MAKE A JOKE ABOUT IT. MANY WOMEN DIDN'T ENJOY IT AND NEVER HAD AN ORGASM . . .
MEN BACK THEN DIDN'T KNOW HOW TO RESTRAIN THEMSELVES, AND THEY'D JUST GRAB GIRLS WHENEVER THEY FELT LIKE IT . . . THE POOR GIRLS NEVER HAD AN ORGASM BECAUSE BEFORE THEY'D EVEN GOTTEN WARMED UP, THE GUYS WOULD ALREADY BE FINISHING.
AND YOU WERE JUST STUCK WITH IT, TOUGH LUCK!
RINGGG!
Grandma Maruja
HI, GRANDMA! YES, YES, I GOT HOME JUST FINE. I'M AT GRANDMA HERMINIA'S HOUSE NOW, TALKING ABOUT HER STORY.
PASS HER TO ME, I'LL SAY HELLO.

HOW ARE YOU, MARUJA?

HI, HERMINIA. WELL, I'M A BIT SAD RIGHT NOW BECAUSE
ANA LEFT. SHE HARDLY EVER COMES TO VISIT! WE'RE OLD
LADIES, YOU KNOW. NOBODY'S INTERESTED IN US.

YOU HAVE TO BE PATIENT, MARUJA. WE'VE GOT TO
MAKE AS LITTLE TROUBLE AS POSSIBLE.

SURE, SURE, BUT I TOOK SUCH
GOOD CARE OF THEM.

WELL, WE'VE LIVED OUR LIVES. NOW WE GET TO
WATCH THEM LIVE THEIRS.

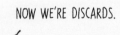

NOW WE'RE DISCARDS.

NOW IS ONLY MOMENTS.

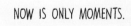

LIFE'S PRETTY DULL, HUH?

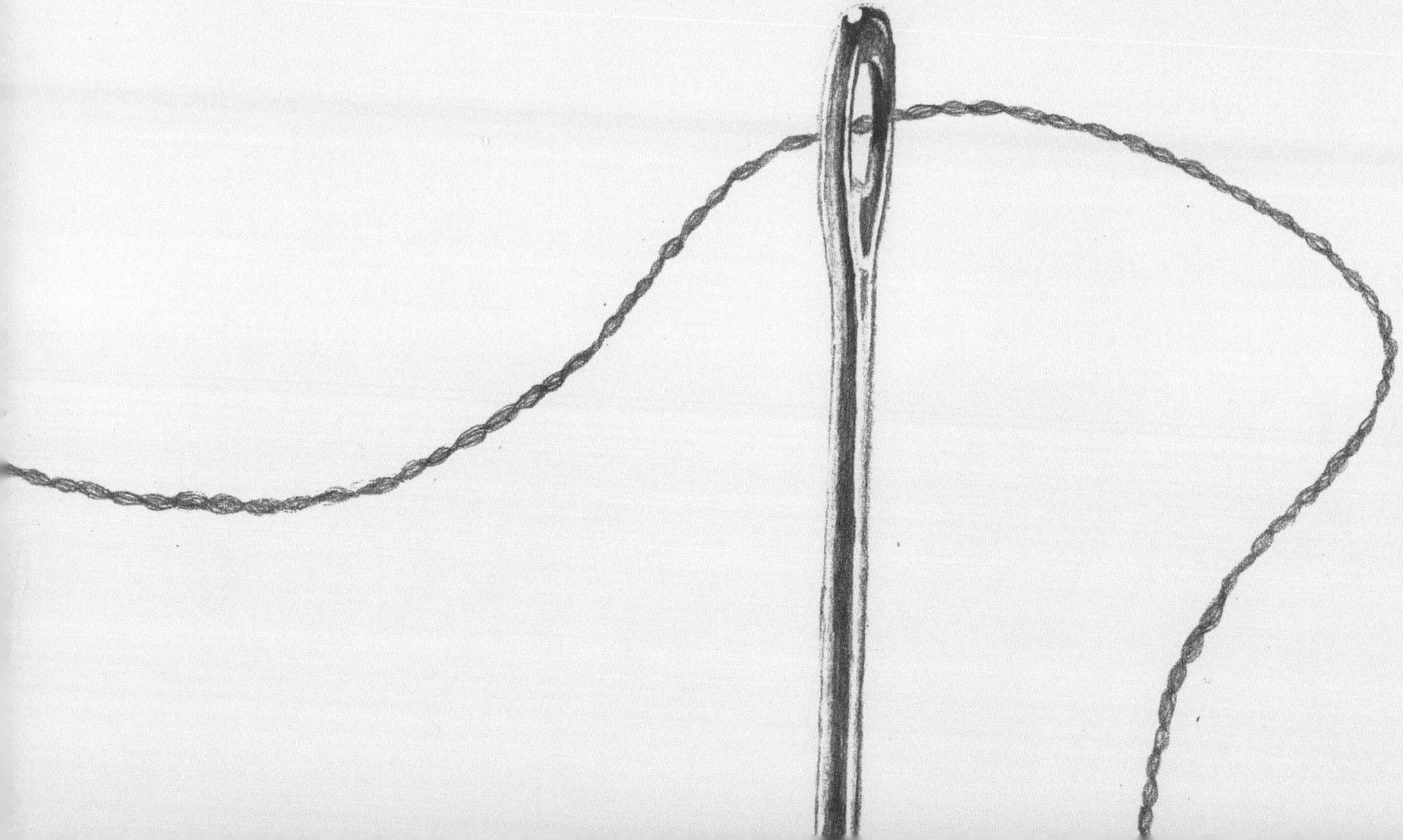

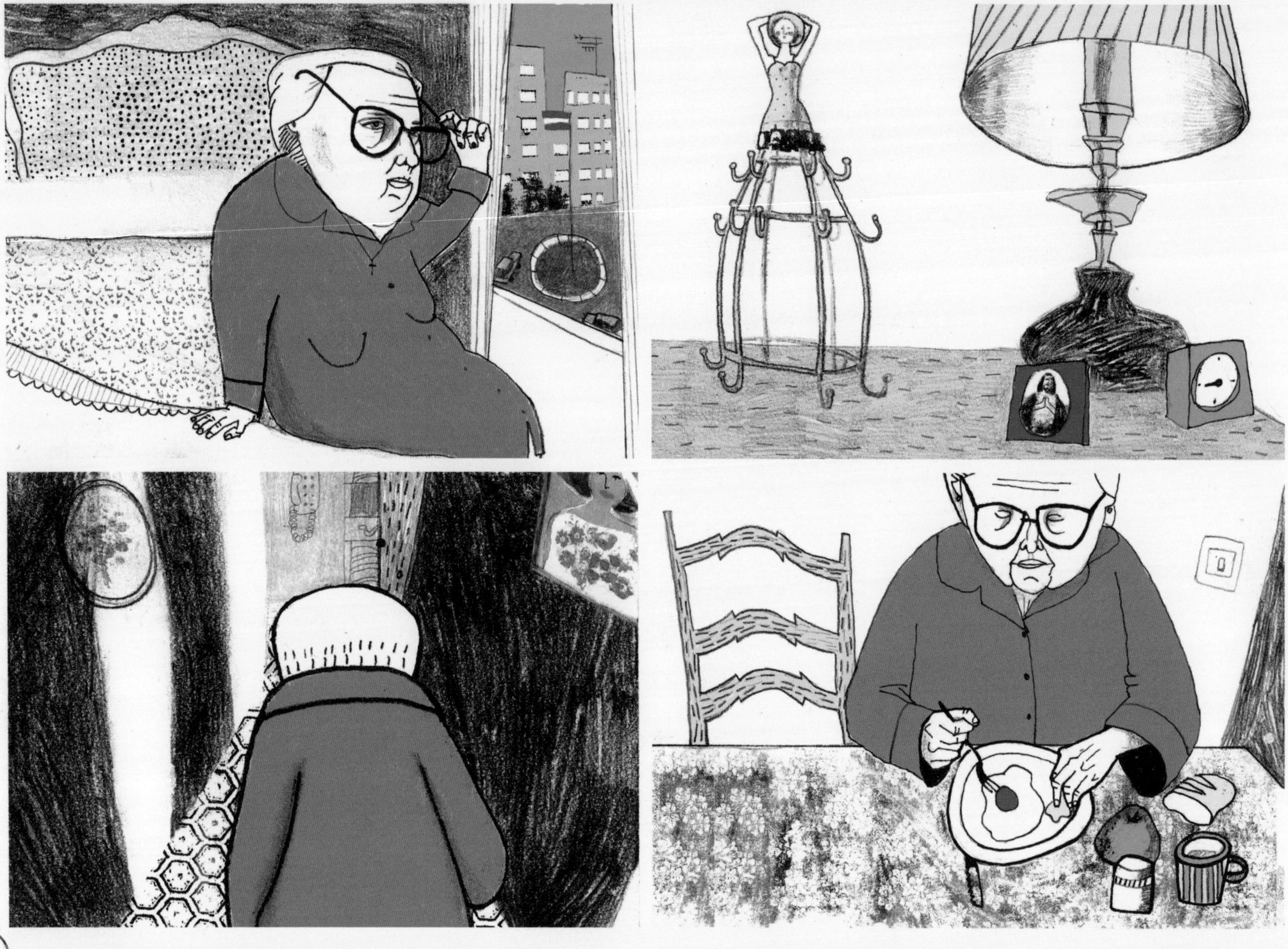

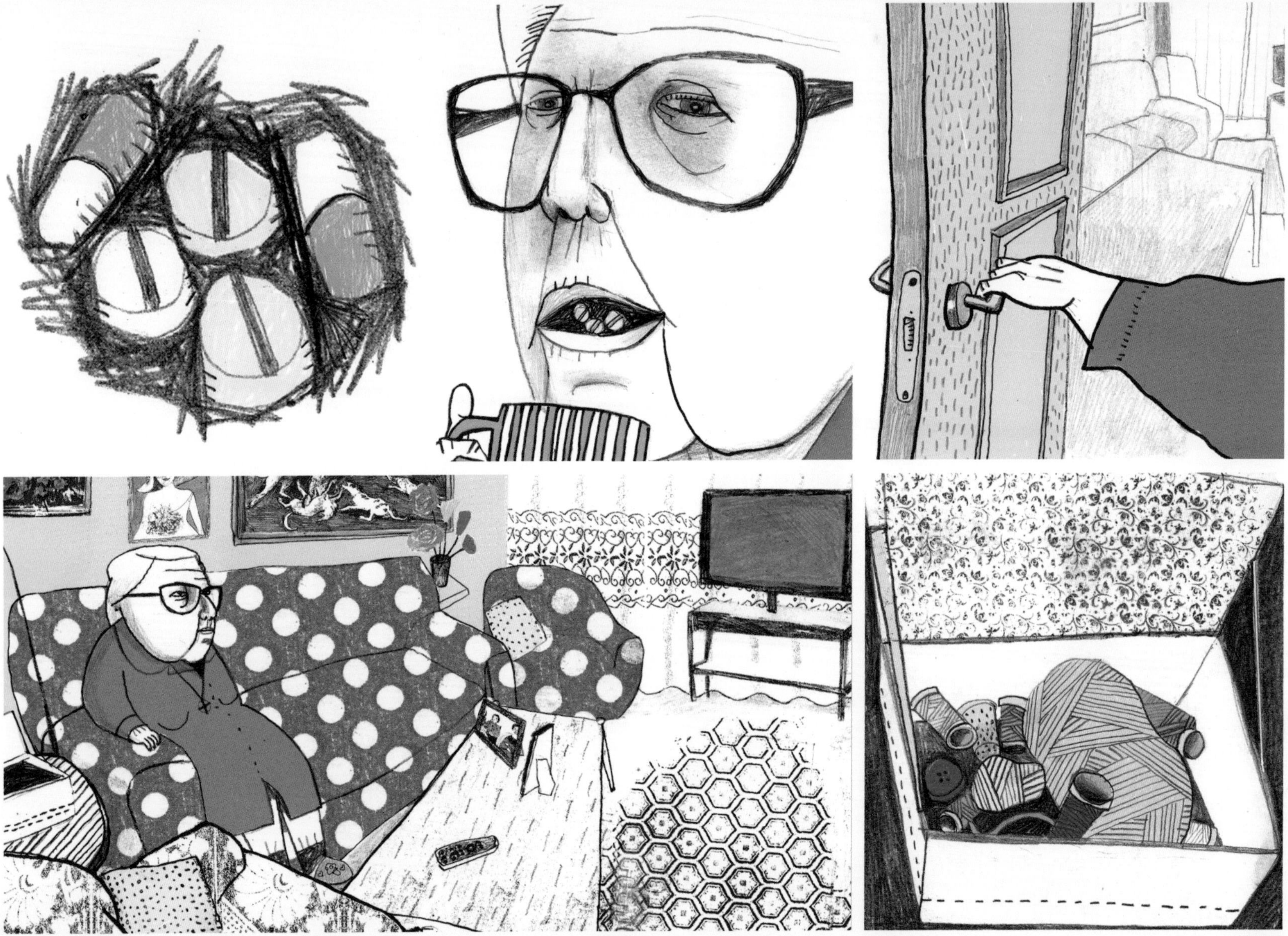

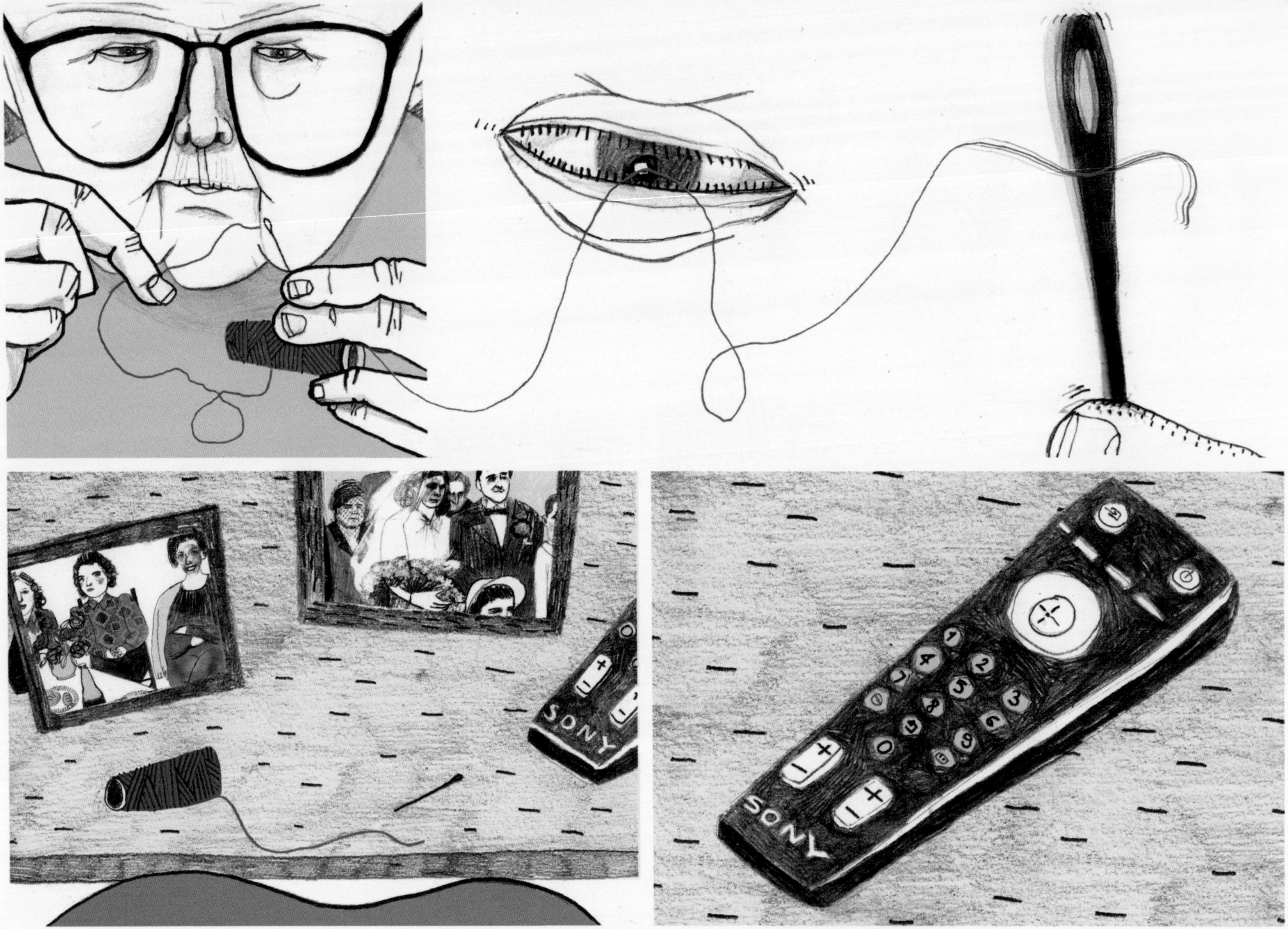
SONY
SONY

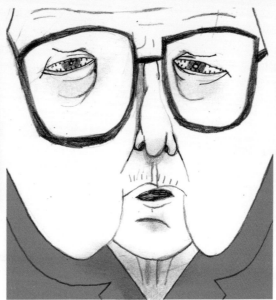

[CDMNG IESDEFCHNS FUFNWEDCX]

[MESSI DRIBBLES TO THE RIGHT!]

[AMAZING! SPOTLESS!]

[THEY HATE YOU BOTH WITH A PASSION.]

I'VE NEVER INSULTED HIS FATHER OR MOTHER; THEY'RE THE ONES WHO REFUSE TO RESPECT MY DAUGHTER AND ME.

YOU TELL 'EM!

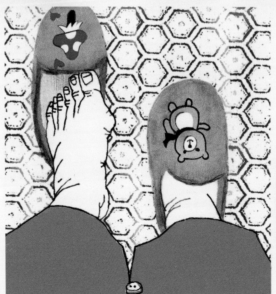

HI, GRANDMA, HOW ARE YOU?

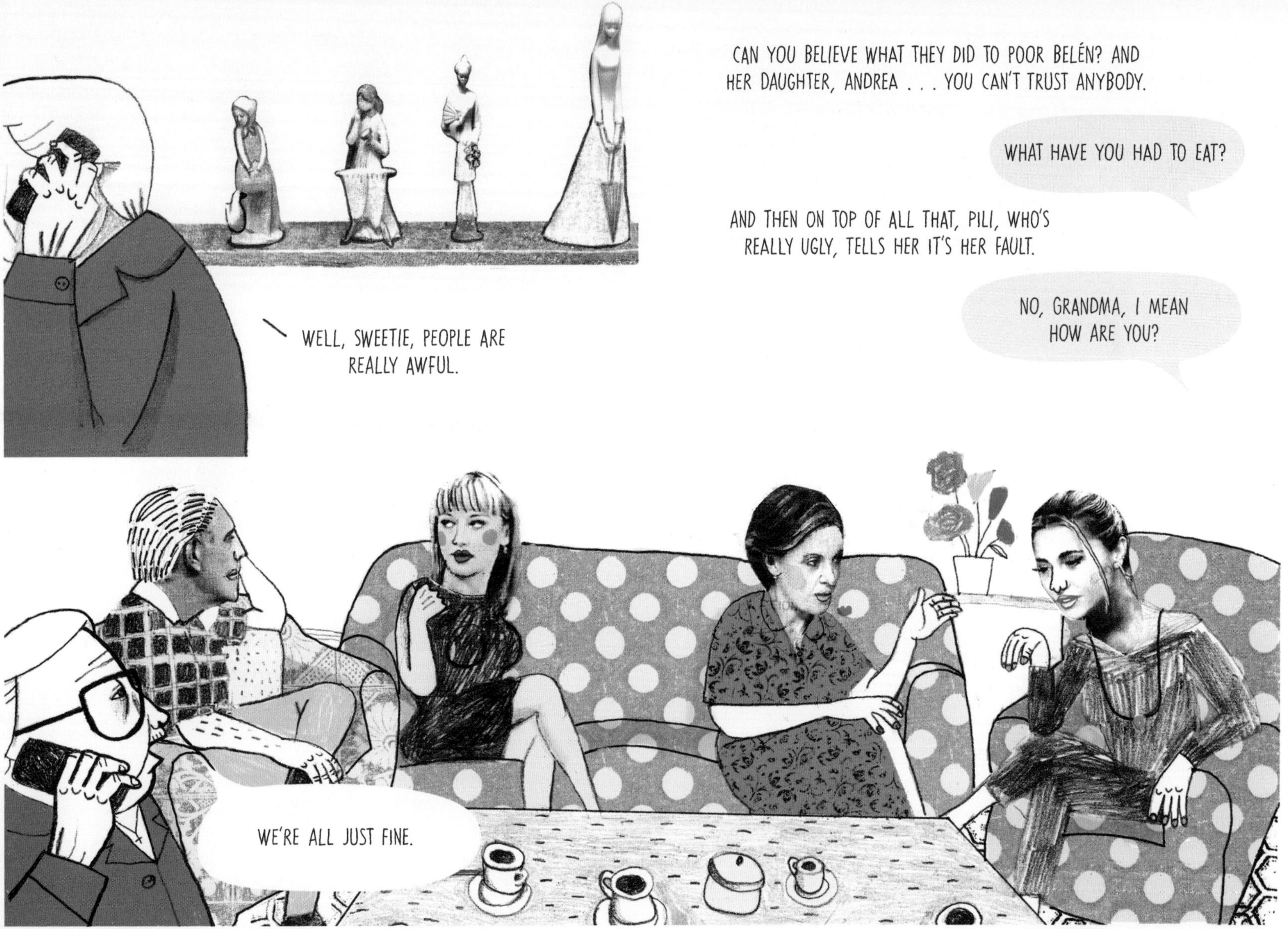
CAN YOU BELIEVE WHAT THEY DID TO POOR BELÉN? AND HER DAUGHTER, ANDREA . . . YOU CAN'T TRUST ANYBODY.
WHAT HAVE YOU HAD TO EAT?
AND THEN ON TOP OF ALL THAT, PILI, WHO'S REALLY UGLY, TELLS HER IT'S HER FAULT.
NO, GRANDMA, I MEAN HOW ARE YOU?
WELL, SWEETIE, PEOPLE ARE REALLY AWFUL.
WE'RE ALL JUST FINE.

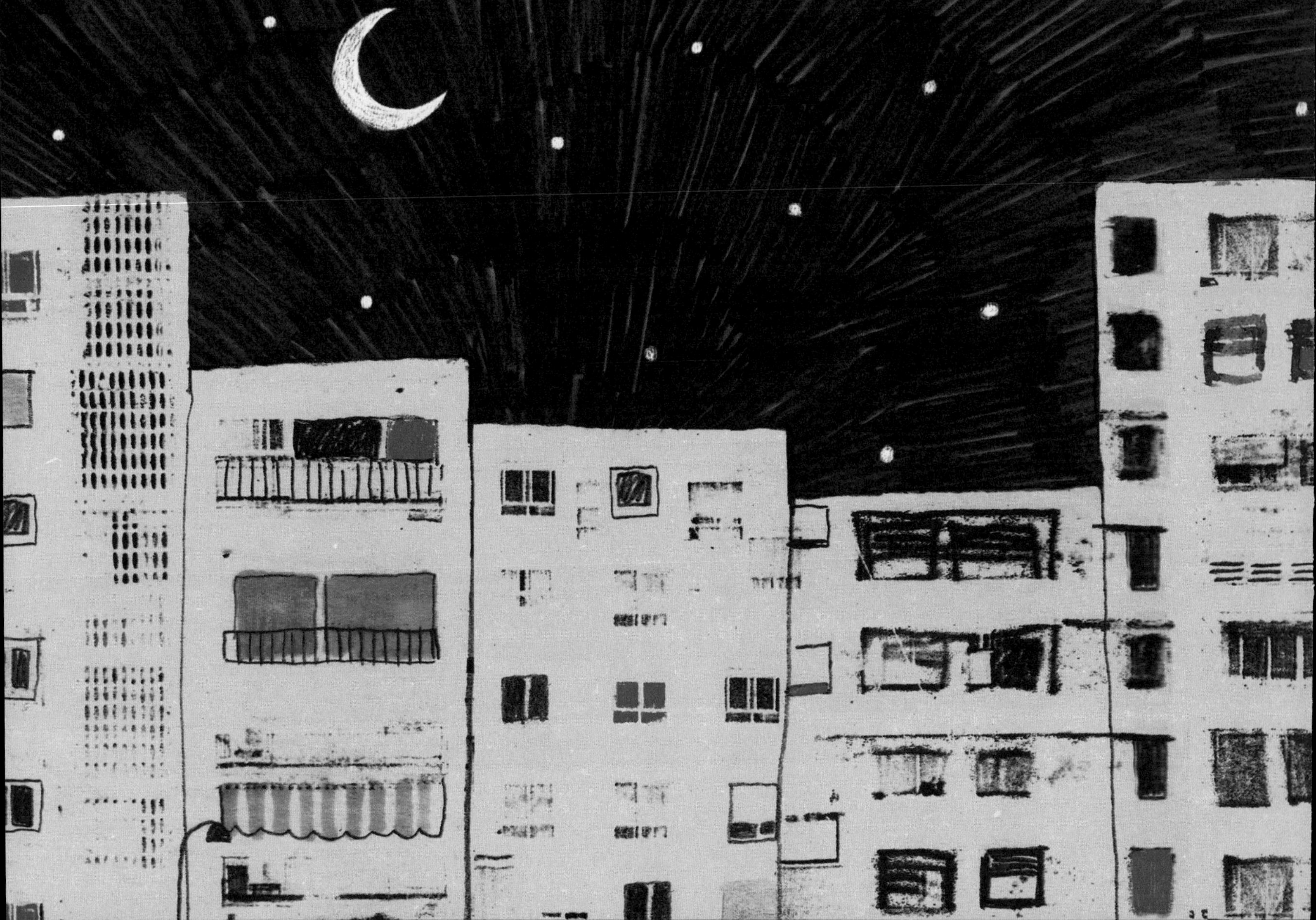

Afterword

by Esther Claudio

IN 2018, ANA PENYAS BECAME THE FIRST WOMAN TO WIN THE NATIONAL COMIC AWARD IN SPAIN FOR *ESTAMOS TODAS BIEN* (*WE'RE ALL JUST FINE*), A BEAUTIFULLY CRAFTED WORK THAT BRINGS TO LIGHT HER TWO GRANDMOTHERS' MEMORIES OF STRUGGLE DURING GENERAL FRANCISCO FRANCO'S DICTATORSHIP (1939-75). AMPLIFYING THE VOICES OF THE SURVIVORS OF FRANCOISM HAS BEEN CENTRAL TO SPAIN'S TRANSITIONAL JUSTICE, BUT THESE PERSPECTIVES REMAIN LIMITED WHEN WORKS BY, FOR AND ABOUT WOMEN ARE THE EXCEPTION. IN THIS GRAPHIC NOVEL, PENYAS INTERWEAVES THE SWEET AND TENDER MEMORIES OF HER GRANDMOTHERS INTO A SOCIALLY CONSCIOUS NARRATIVE ABOUT THREE GENERATIONS OF WOMEN WHO REFUSED TO BELIEVE THAT THEY "WERE ALL JUST FINE."

HERMINIA AND MARUJA'S EXPERIENCES OF FRANCO'S DICTATORSHIP PROVIDE AN INTIMATE GLIMPSE INTO LIFE IN A SURVEILLANCE STATE. THE *GUARDIA CIVIL* (CIVIL GUARD), THE MILITARY POLICE THAT SUPPORTED THE FASCIST CAUSE THROUGH INTIMIDATION AND VIOLENCE, LOOMS MENACINGLY IN THEIR MEMORIES. WHEN YOUNG MARUJA IS LEFT ALONE TO CLOSE DOWN THE BAR AT NIGHT (P. 15), SHE FEARS FOR HER PHYSICAL SAFETY UPON SEEING ONE OF ITS MEMBERS. LATER ON, A YOUNG HERMINIA LOOKS WITH CONCERN AT THE SIGHT OF A CIVIL GUARD INTERROGATION ON THE SIDE OF THE ROAD (P. 49). THE PRESENCE OF CIVIL GUARDS IN THE STORY REVEALS LARGER

DYNAMICS OF INSTITUTIONALIZED OPPRESSION IN A REGIME THAT CONSTITUTED A FATAL BLOW TO WOMEN'S LIBERTIES.

ANA PENYAS'S MOTHER, MARIBEL CHUMILLAS, WAS AT THE FOREFRONT OF SPAIN'S FIGHT AGAINST FASCISM. MARIBEL'S MEMBERSHIP CARD OF THE OUTLAWED "WORKER'S VOICE," A LEFTIST STUDENT GROUP, INTRODUCES ONE OF THE CHAPTERS DEVOTED TO HER MOTHER, HERMINIA (P. 58). HERE, WE LEARN THAT HERMINIA HIDES "SUBVERSIVE" BOOKS LIKE WILHELM REICH'S *THE FUNCTION OF THE ORGASM* TO KEEP HER DAUGHTER SAFE FROM THE WATCHFUL EYES OF THE REGIME. MARIBEL ENJOYS AN EDUCATION AND SOME LIBERTIES THAT BUILD ON HER OWN MOTHER'S LIMITATIONS. IN A PREVIOUS SCENE, HERMINIA APPEARS CONFINED TO ONE ROOM OF THE HOUSE, CONSTANTLY KEPT BUSY CLEANING WHILE HER DAUGHTER AND THE REST OF HER FAMILY, IN THE FOREGROUND, COME AND GO AND LIVE THEIR LIVES (P. 56). IN *WE'RE ALL JUST FINE*, EACH CHAPTER IS INTRODUCED WITH SYMBOLS OF DOMESTIC LABOR (A POT, A LAUNDRY BASKET, AN APRON, ETC.) — THE ONLY EXCEPTION BEING MARIBEL'S CARD AND THE FACE OF THE SPANISH QUEEN LETIZIA, WHICH INTRODUCES A CHAPTER ABOUT MARRIAGE AND APPEARANCES (P. 33). THIS FOCUS ON DOMESTIC OBJECTS UNDERSCORES THE UNDERVALUED NATURE OF WOMEN'S UNPAID LABOR AS STAY-AT-HOME MOTHERS. PENYAS SUBTLY DEPICTS HOW EVERYDAY ROUTINES CAN REVEAL HIERARCHICAL DYNAMICS OF DOMINATION AND INEQUALITY.

MARUJA AND HERMINIA WITNESSED A RADICAL TRANSFORMATION OF THE LANDSCAPE IN THE TRANSITION FROM THE DICTATORIAL YEARS TO DEMOCRATIC SPAIN. FOR EXAMPLE, THE BILLBOARDS THAT WELCOMED HERMINIA TO

MADRID IN 1969 ANNOUNCED "GASEOSA 'LA CASERA': FAMILIA GRANDE, BOTELLA GRANDE," A SPANISH SODA IN A BIG BOTTLE FOR THE "BIG FAMILIES" THAT THE FASCIST IDEAL PROMOTED (P. 50). RIGHT BESIDE IT, THE ADVERTISEMENT FOR "JABÓN LAGARTO," A PARTICULARLY HARSH SOAP FOR WASHING LAUNDRY BY HAND, IS PAIRED WITH THE "NIVEA CREAM" TO ENSURE THE HOUSEWIFE HAD PERFECTLY SOFT HANDS FOR HER HUSBAND. A DECADE LATER, MARUJA VISITS DEMOCRATIC MADRID DURING THE YEARS OF *LA MOVIDA* (THE CULTURAL BOOM THAT FLOURISHED AFTER THE DEATH OF THE DICTATOR) AND OBSERVES THE BILLBOARDS ANNOUNCING PEDRO ALMODÓVAR'S DEBUT FILM, *PEPI, LUCI, BOM Y OTRAS CHICAS DEL MONTÓN*, WHICH FEATURES THREE WOMEN IN REBELLIOUS ATTITUDE AND PUNK AESTHETICS (P. 71). IN SHARP CONTRAST WITH THE BILLBOARDS THAT IMPOSED AN IMPOSSIBLE IDEAL OF HOUSEWIFE TO HERMINIA A DECADE

AGO, ALMODÓVAR'S FILM DEPICTS A NEW TYPE OF WOMAN THAT MARUJA CANNOT IDENTIFY WITH BUT WHO REPRESENTS THE MODERN, LIBERATED YOUTH. THROUGH SUBTLE DETAILS LIKE THESE, *WE'RE ALL JUST FINE* CLUES THE READER IN ON THE SOCIOCULTURAL TRANSFORMATIONS THAT HERMINIA AND MARUJA OBSERVE AROUND THEM.

WE'RE ALL JUST FINE PLACES GREAT EMPHASIS ON THE VISUAL, ON WHAT GOES UNSAID, ON THE DETAILS THAT ADDRESS THE UNIVERSAL THROUGH THE LOCAL. CHARACTERS COMMUNICATE THROUGH GAZES, SLIGHT GESTURES, SILENCES. FOR EXAMPLE, IN THE SCENE OF THE *PEPI, LUCI, BOM* POSTER, MARUJA'S EYES IN HER CAR'S REAR VIEW MIRROR ARE JUXTAPOSED OVER THE DEPICTION OF TWO NONBINARY PEOPLE THAT LOOK LIKE ALMODÓVAR AND SINGER FABIO MCNAMARA. A NEW REALITY OPENS BEFORE HER EYES AND THE READER WITNESSES THESE SOCIETAL SHIFTS THROUGH

MARUJA'S PERSPECTIVE — BUT HOW SHE INTERPRETS THEM IS LEFT AMBIGUOUS. AT ANOTHER POINT IN THE STORY, ANA PENYAS'S ALTER EGO OBSERVES THE CLUTTER OF POTS AND PANS ACCUMULATED IN HER GRANDMA HERMINIA'S SINK (P. 85). ANA WANTS TO HELP CLEAN UP BUT HERMINIA INSISTS SHE WILL DO IT, REVEALING HOW PENYAS HERSELF IS COMPLICIT IN THE VERY DYNAMICS THAT THE COMIC CRITICIZES. VISUALLY, PENYAS'S USE OF PHOTO COLLAGE AND A RED AND BROWN COLOR PALETTE RECALL RUSSIAN CONSTRUCTIVISM'S SPIRIT OF SOCIAL CHANGE. THE SHATTERED GEOMETRIC PERSPECTIVE OF MOST PANELS RESEMBLES THE WORK OF POST-EXPRESSIONISTS SUCH AS OTTO DIX, WHO REJECTED ROMANTIC IDEALISM IN THEIR PORTRAYAL OF STRUCTURAL INEQUALITIES. WITH THE SAME COMMITMENT TO SOCIAL JUSTICE, PENYAS DESCRIBES HER GRANDMOTHERS' SOLITUDE AS PART OF LARGER DYNAMICS OF OPPRESSION AND EMANCIPATION. *WE'RE ALL JUST FINE* DEMANDS THE READER TO PAY CLOSE ATTENTION TO AN ARRAY OF SEEMINGLY MUNDANE DETAILS AND SYMBOLS TO UNCOVER THE DEEPER MEANINGS THEY EVOKE.

THE MEMORIES OF HERMINIA AND MARUJA DO NOT SPEAK OF GREAT DEEDS, OF HISTORICAL EVENTS OR OF PUBLIC LIFE. INSTEAD, THEY SPEAK OF THE EVERYDAY, OF DOMESTICITY, OF THE ETHICS OF CARE. THROUGH DEPICTIONS OF HOUSEHOLD LABOR, THE DOMESTIC IMAGERY OF FABRICS, SCRAPS AND THREADS, ANA PENYAS PIECES TOGETHER SPAIN'S TRANSITION FROM FRANCOISM INTO CONTEMPORARY CONSUMERIST SOCIETY AND GIVES VOICE TO HER GRANDMOTHERS AND THE GENERATION OF MARGINALIZED WOMEN THEY REPRESENT. *WE'RE ALL JUST FINE* TRANSFORMS THE THREAD WITH WHICH MARUJA SEEMS TO HAVE "SPENT [HER] WHOLE LIFE MENDING THE BEDSHEETS" INTO A TOOL FOR EMPATHY, JUSTICE AND CHANGE.

End Notes

i: WRITER CARMEN MARTÍN GAITE (1925–2000) WAS CENTRAL TO REVITALIZING SPANISH LITERATURE IN THE POST-CIVIL WAR YEARS. ADEPT IN MANY GENRES, SHE WAS PARTICULARLY KNOWN FOR HER NOVELS THAT EXPLORED THE INNER LIVES OF VIBRANT WOMEN CHARACTERS. THIS QUOTE FROM HER BOOK *COURTSHIP CUSTOMS IN POSTWAR SPAIN* (1987) INCISIVELY COMPARES THE GENERATION OF POSTWAR WOMEN TO ODYSSEUS'S WIFE PENELOPE, WHO WEAVES AS SHE WAITS FOR HIM TO RETURN FROM HIS ADVENTURES.

15–16: THIS SCENE DEPICTS THE *GUARDIA CIVIL*, FRANCO'S MILITARY POLICE FORCE, WHICH PATROLLED SPAIN'S COUNTRY TOWNS AND RURAL AREAS AND ENFORCED STRICT SOCIAL CONTROL THROUGH OFTEN VIOLENT, SUPPRESSIVE MEANS. THE *GUARDIA CIVIL*'S MENACING OMNIPRESENCE CAN ALSO BE SEEN IN THE ROADSIDE SCENE ON PAGE 57.

33–34: THESE DEPICTIONS OF QUEEN LETIZIA OF SPAIN HIGHLIGHT THE IDEA THAT, SIMILARLY TO THE QUEEN, THE AUTHOR'S GRANDMA MARUJA FEELS THAT SHE PLAYED THE ROLE OF TROPHY WIFE IN HER MARRIAGE.

48: ORIGINAL SPANISH LYRICS:

UN RAYO DE SOL,
¡OH, OH, OH!

—"UN RAYO DE SOL" BY LOS DIABLOS (1970)

THE LIGHTHEARTED NATURE OF THIS BOUNCY POP SONG PROVIDES AN IRONIC CONTRAST WITH THE SORROW THE AUTHOR'S GRANDMA HERMINIA FEELS AS HER FAMILY IS UPROOTED IN THIS SCENE.